RAFFI
(Hagob Melik Hagobian, cir. 1835-1888)

TAJKAHAYK
(THE ARMENIAN QUESTION)

translated by
Ara Stepan Melkonian

Gomidas Institute
London

GOMIDAS INSTITUTE - ARMENIAN LITERATURE IN TRANSLATION

Published by Taderon Press by special arrangement with the Gomidas Institute.

New edition, Gomidas Institute, 2021.

© 2007 Garod Books Ltd. All Rights Reserved.

ISBN 978-1-909382-59-6

Gomidas Institute
42 Blythe Rd.
London, W14 0HA
ENGLAND
Email: *info@gomidas.org*
Web: *www.gomidas.org*

TABLE OF CONTENTS

INTRODUCTION	v
TRANSLATOR'S NOTE (Ara Stepan Melkonian)	ix
NOTE (from Anna Raffi, 1910)	1
WHAT LINK IS THERE BETWEEN US AND THE ARMENIANS IN TURKEY?	3
REPORT	23
WHAT ARE THE REFORMS NEEDED IN TURKISH ARMENIA?	61
THE KURDISH UNION	71
THE KURD AND THE TURK	85
THE ESCAPE ROUTE	93
LET US HELP	96

Introduction

This translation of *Tajkahayk* by Raffi (Hagop Melik Hagopian, 1835-1888) is made up of eight articles written between 1877 and 1880 on the on the social, political and economic conditions of Armenians in the Ottoman Empire. Five of these articles were printed in the newspaper *Mshak* during Raffi's lifetime and three were printed posthumously in compilations of *Tajkahayk*. To date there have been three major editions of *Tajkahayk* published in Tiflis (1895), Vienna (1895) and Vienna (1913).[1]

According to Donald Abcarian, a specialist on Raffi, these editions of *Tajkahayk* were probably published as a response to the Hamidian massacres of 1894-96, and the further development of the Armenian Question prior to WWI, to "bring to the fore the history that led to these defining moments in Ottoman Armenian history and to offer some intelligent basis for salvation. *Tajkahayk* was therefore a work with a very concrete political goal, not just a literary exercise. In this context, the apparent irrelevance of the last section on Jerusalem [first appearing in the 1913 edition] is not as it may seem, since it was a call to stop squandering national wealth on pilgrimages, which only fed the corrupt and ravenous church, instead of contributing to the defence of the Armenian homeland."[2] The present translation is based on the Vienna 1913 text but omits the chapter on Jerusalem.

Today *Tajkahayk* could be read as part of Ottoman Armenian social, intellectual and political history, in which Raffi reflected on pressing issues concerning Armenians in the mid-1870s. The core of *Tajkahayk* concerned the problem of the depredations suffered by the Armenian peasantry in the provinces. His exposition of this issue entailed the detailed presentation of data and analysis. Raffi gathered most of his information from the Ottoman Armenian press and publications of the Armenian National Administration in

---

1 The Vienna edition was the most extensive one by including the two additional chapters of "Let Us Help" and "Jerusalem..."
2 Donald Abcarian to Ara Sarafian private correspondence.

Constantinople. Raffi thus probed, engaged and helped to integrate a new discourse regarding the position of Armenians in the Ottoman Empire. The fact that he presented his assessment in *Mshak,* a much respected newspaper, added to the potency of his views. Raffi's writing had far-reaching consequences, and even today *Tajkahayk* makes compelling reading.

Raffi's views as expressed in *Tajkahayk* had enormous consequences because they fed into the political consciousness and radicalized opinion amongst Armenians. This radicalization took place as a result of the Ottoman authorities' continued failure to respond to public petitions concerning the depredations and injustice faced by Armenians. A major watershed in these developments was the defeat of the Ottoman Empire in the Russo-Turkish War of 1877-78, when Russian armies occupied much of the so-called Armenian provinces in the Ottoman Empire. Armenian community leaders sent a delegation to the European powers to compel the Ottoman government to implement reforms, and they requested that the Russian withdrawal from the Armenian provinces should be linked to the introduction of reforms guaranteeing the security of life and property in the provinces in question.[3] The intellectual background to these developments was set in the 1870s, when the question of provincial depredations and misrule had already been articulated as matters of grave concern by Armenian intellectuals such as Raffi.

The Ottoman authorities under Abdul Hamid II (1878-1908) and then the Committee of Union and Progress (1908-1918) did not respond to either internal or external pressures to ameliorate the condition of Armenians in the Ottoman Empire. The continuing failure of the Ottoman authorities to address what now came to be known as the Armenian Question led to the formation of Armenian revolutionary organizations in the 1890s. Organized state violence against the Armenian population of the Ottoman Empire culminated in the Hamidian massacres of 1895-96, the Adana massacres of 1909, and the Armenian genocide of 1915.

---

3 These demands were made in Article 16 of the Treaty of San Stefano (1878) and article 61 of the Treaty of Berlin (1878).

Today Raffi's *Tajkahayk* can be read for its invaluable insight into the social and intellectual origins of the Armenian Question, as well as for a better understanding of Raffi's more literary works, such as *The Fool* and *Jalaleddin,* which championed the emancipation of the Ottoman Armenian peasantry.

Translator's Note

This translation has been rendered from the 1983 edition published by Armen publishing house in Tehran, Iran. It should be noted that some items quoted by the original editor in the "Note" do not appear in it.

I have not included the final item of the 1983 edition, namely a section concerning the Armenian monastery in Jerusalem that was a separate article; it is excluded here, as it has nothing directly to do with the subject of Armenians in Turkey.

All the italics used in the text are those of the author; none are added for emphasis.

The footnotes marked (see "Author's note") are those from the original Armenian text; they were inserted by either the author or the original editor. I have added all the others as clarifications to the text.

Any errors in rendering the original text are solely my responsibility.

Finally, I would like to insert a word of thanks to three people: Ara Sarafian, of the Gomidas Institute, who asked me to undertake this translation, my friend Don Abcarian who read and commented on it, and to my wife Anne, who is always a constant source of help and encouragement in my efforts to render Armenian texts into English, and thus make them accessible to a wider audience.

Ara Stepan Melkonian
Hordle, 2005

TAJKAHAYK
(THE ARMENIAN QUESTION)

Note
[to the 1910 publication]

This is the first time that the articles "Armenia Between Two Fires" and its preface "We Are Deluding Ourselves with Hope"—both of which are included in this book—have been published. It is true that the article "We Are Being Deceived by Empty Hopes" appeared in *Mshag* in 187[9], but that was a brief sketch that was not even published in its complete form. The following is what *Mshag*'s[1] secretary at that time, H. Der-Krikorian, wrote in his letter to the author (dated February 24) who was, at that time, in Akoulis:

Your articles are much read, especially the one printed in *Mshag* number 22, from which the "undertaker of minds" (the censor) removed much, but we must be thankful for what's been left.

The article created a great impression—especially in literary circles, but also among the general reading public; the excitement was generated by the new ideas it stirred up, despite the censor's excisions.

The author of the letter continues:

K. Ardzrouni has thanked me many times for publishing the article. "We Are Being Deceived by Empty Hopes" left a special impression.

Encouraged by these letters and other sympathetic feelings concerning the article, the author expanded it with the aim of bringing his theoretical understanding as close as possible to our times. Unfortunately, he did not write about more recent times. There are, however, draft pieces and subjects that the author wanted to use to create the history of later times. Comparing them with great

---

1. *Mshag* [Cultivator] was an Armenian periodical published in Tbilisi, Georgia in the latter half of the 19th century.

care, we have appended some of the draft pieces to the completed work as notes, in each case adding "notes to the subject".[2]

The author partly completes his theory by examining the subject and other points of view in passing; they are noted in parentheses in *Samvel*.[3] The assertion that purely historical theory had a special significance in our literature brought about a new reading of history.

Many historical writings have subsequently appeared by various authors, based on Raffi's new readings of history.

The Melikdoms of Khamsa,[4] *Tavit Beg*[5] and *Samvel* are rich historical storehouses written in a new critical spirit.

We have brought together all these parts to complete Raffi's historical theories. We did not consider it superfluous to add a brief piece to them, namely "A Conversation Between Sahag and Mesrob" from *Samvel*, which concerns the same subject seen from a different angle.[6] Tavit Beg forms the "latest era": it is a small historical theory piece that the author wrote before the novel of the same name; it has, until now, remained unpublished.

Widow Anna Raffi

London, November 2, 1910

---

2. The edition we used as the source document for this translation only has footnotes without any distinguishing annotations. We have marked these with "(Author's note)". Our own annotations simply appear as footnotes.
3. *Samvel* (Samuel) by Raffi is a historical novel set in 5th century Armenia. It was first published in 1888, just before the author's death.
4. *The Melikdoms of Khamsa* by Raffi is a historical survey of the Armenian principalities of Karabagh (Artsakh), first published in 1882.
5. *Tavit Beg* by Raffi is a historical novel concerning the events of the 18th century in Karabagh (Artsakh).
6. Both of these sections have been omitted from the edition used for this translation. We are currently working on a translation of both novels in their entirety.

WHAT LINK IS THERE BETWEEN US AND THE ARMENIANS IN TURKEY?[7]

1

Until the last Russo-Turkish war, if a Turkish Armenian were seen in our parts with a fez on his head, he would immediately have been called "hosos"[8] and we would have turned our faces away from him. Even our children would call the farm labourers from Van and Moush "gouro",[9] and many were convinced that "gouros" were not Armenian, but from one or another Kurdish tribe.

The Armenians from Turkey had the same kind of false and strange ideas about us. If one of us were to be seen in the streets of Constantinople or another city, Turkish Armenians would cast a suspicious glance at us and, commenting that "He's one of them," they would point him out to their friends. They considered us to be estranged from Armenian identity. We did not recognise one another—they were hateful toward us and we toward them.

All communications between us were cut; trade—which could have created better relations between us—did not exist. Turkish Armenians traded with Europeans, and our merchants traded with Moscow and Nijna [Nijni-Novgorod]. A few of their tobacco sellers have only recently appeared in Tbilisi.

There remain only two things that could introduce us to one another: literature and the press.

---

7. "Inch Gab", *Mshak*, 1879.
8. *Hosos*: a derogatory term for Turkish Armenians.
9. *Gouro* or *gero*: this could be translated as 'bumpkin'.

But do we really have a literature? We have, indeed, an ancient and rich classical literature, but nothing at all that is new. By reading Yeghishe, we can obtain information about how the Armenians of the fifth century were tortured by the Persians, but nothing in literature today tells us about the current state of Armenians in Turkey.

It is possible to get to know nations or peoples through their literature, even without seeing them, but only when that literature is the perfect expression of their life and intellectual strength—when their economic, industrial and social life, their thought and aspirations and, in a word, all the varied aspects of their existence find expression in it. Both we and our Armenian brothers in Turkey are bereft of such a literature.

What was the press doing?

Our press did not concern itself with the people in Turkey in the past, or even with our local issues or life. The Armenian press in Turkey is in the same poor condition today as ours was 10 years ago.

I am convinced that if someone were to carefully study all the issues of *Mshag* or *Meghou*[10] (the new publication), he'd get at least a basic idea of the lives of Russian Armenians, if not a perfect one. He'd cull information about their economic situation, education and culture, and he would also find out how much they have progressed, or what role they have played in trade. He'd also see statistics about how many people live in various regions and so on. By contrast, the press in Constantinople could not provide us with any such information about Armenians living there, as it has not been concerned with local questions. The Constantinople press has been focused on Europe and the intrigues of the Patriarchate, but it has not seen much on the other side of the Bosphorus, in Asia Minor. The state of Armenians living in Armenia and their relationships with their non-Armenian neighbours has not interested the press of Constantinople, and so they have only occasionally printed news of some scandal or other in the provinces and nothing else.

The Constantinople press has not even examined the ground beneath its feet—Constantinople itself. We do not even know the goings-on of the approximately 100,000 Armenians living in the

---

10. *Meghou* (Bee): a contemporary periodical that appeared in Tbilisi at that time.

capital of Turkey; only a few distorted, incorrect and downright false pieces of information have reached us about them from the foreign press, while Constantinople itself has always remained silent about them.

Between 10 and 15—or even more—different kinds of periodicals are published in Constantinople and, setting aside the poverty of their content, there have been no press exchanges between us. Therefore the press has remained incapable of fully introducing us to each other. Feeling the importance of bringing us together *Mshag*—from its first day of publication, and especially in the last few years—has frequently written about the Armenians in Turkey; I am convinced *Mshag* provides readers in Constantinople with the ability to glean more accurate information about Armenians in Asia Minor than in all of their own journals put together.

We knew as much about the situation of Armenians in Turkey as that of the natives of central Africa. Even the Armenians of Constantinople did not know more than we did. The truth of what I am saying is supported by the fact that an Armenian news representative is already in London and another in St. Petersburg, while in Constantinople they have only just realised that they need detailed and accurate information about Armenia; they have sent some monks there, post-haste, to see how many Armenians there are, where they are and what links they have with non-Armenians.[11] It was only at that point that they decided to prepare a map of Armenia, even though there was a Patriarchate in Constantinople, a National Assembly, and an Armenian intelligentsia who should have known about and prepared for all this well in advance, with their principal tool being the press.

It would be unnecessary to cite a further example other than the following: at the time of the Congress of Berlin, the position of the Armenians in Constantinople could be likened to that of a merchant who wishes to enter upon some grand commercial venture but does not first take stock of his finances, and only discovers after the affair

---

11. Raffi is referring to a number of Armenian clergymen who were sent to the provinces of the Ottoman Empire, in the aftermath of the Russo-Turkish war of 1877-78, to gather vital statistics about the Armenian population of western (or Turkish) Armenia.

has run its course that his coffers are empty. Under such circumstances, failure is a foregone conclusion.

Nonetheless, the lack of success—especially after a great revolution [1876]—in the lives of people and defeat after an unsuccessful war [1877-78] has had consequences: it has made people understand that their condition, mistakes and general ineptness are at the root of their failures. Such knowledge has been sufficient to lead people on a more correct and certain path to achieving their future goals. This has been the only useful development in the unsuccessful Turkish Armenian attempt [to make representations for reforms]. Can the Turkish Armenians learn from that experience? This is the question that must be asked.

In fact, that question facing Armenians is so complex that it is difficult to explain it in one attempt. We can only delve into its main aspects. Indeed, every unsuccessful enterprise in the life of a nation has its benefits, in that those failures make citizens recognise their deficiencies and prepare the ground for a new future; from that self-examination, knowledge is gained. But it is difficult to find in all of humanity a people that knows itself, and whose elite—the educated portion—examines itself, like a doctor would his patients. Members of the elite tell the nation of its faults and needs and, at the same time, the ways by which they can satisfy those needs. They are called by several names (social workers, leaders), and their main weapon is the spoken and written word. They represent the people's intellectual power—its intelligentsia.

At the beginning of this article we questioned whether the poor Turkish Armenian intelligentsia had the capability of taking the lead and exercising the influence required to stir up the masses and raise them from their fallen state.

The condition in the different regions must be taken into account. It is understandable that Constantinople, as an official location, has the Sublime Porte there; the Armenian Patriarchate may always have communication with vizier[12] and the representatives of the European powers there. But Constantinople is not suitable as the centre of energies concerned with Armenia; although it contains the leading Turkish Armenian people, the city cannot really affect distant

---

12. In this case the author means government ministers, appointed by the Sultan.

Armenia from its isolated position. There are seas between it and Turkish Armenia and the Anatolian landmass, even without bringing into the issue the bad state of communication by road. For all these reasons, one may understand the little influence that the people of Constantinople can exert on those in the real Armenia. It is not possible, therefore, to hope for everything from the people of Constantinople or to expect everything from them alone.

We Russian Armenians, more than the Armenians of Constantinople, can help the Armenians in Turkey, as we have close neighbourly contacts with them. That aside, the Russian Armenian is relatively better off than those of Constantinople, both intellectually and financially. Why are we leaving everything to the people of Constantinople? We should share the problems of our brothers who are being crushed by the yoke of tyranny.

The recovery of Armenians in Turkey must always be considered suspect, if hope is placed exclusively on Constantinople. Assistance should be given by all Armenians, wherever they may be, and especially by us, the Russian Armenians. Fortunately our benevolent government does not forbid us to help them; on the contrary, it would like us to prepare the people in Asia Minor to be a shield against British influence. It would like Christian people to be freed from Turkish tyranny, for so much of its Russian soldiers' blood has been spilt in that cause.

What can we do? This is the question that may be asked by the reader. Much can be done, but only if we actively think about helping.

Before providing assistance, however, it is necessary to understand the needs of the Turkish Armenians and to establish contact and relations with them in whatever way possible. It is not enough for us to be neighbours, as our neighbourliness has been such that we have not had the opportunity to know one another. As noted at the beginning of our article, there is not—nor has there been—any unifying link between us and the Turkish Armenians.

There is only one link between us and that is kinship: we both belong to the same nation, speak the same language, and the same blood flows in our veins. There is one other link, and that is religion: we both belong to the same Church. This last link can hardly be said to be complete, due to various divisions—including our Catholic, Protestant and Muslim brothers separating from us—and it is loose even for the Armenian Apostolic Church as, for our sins, our Church's governments are in two opposing countries: Turkey and Russia. It seems that there are two opposing thrones,[13] a situation that became even more obvious during the latest political events [of 1878], when the Catholicosate of Holy Etchmiadzin[14] kept itself in deaf indifference—or at least did not join in the hopes of the Patriarch of Constantinople. History will, of course, condemn that great indifference, while honest people living today cannot observe it without deep disquiet.

It must be confessed with sadness that, without taking into account all of our hopes, the recent election of the Catholicos of All Armenians by the churchmen from Turkey did not justify the hope that the Catholicos of All Armenians, elected from Turkey, would improve the links of Holy Etchmiadzin with the Patriarchate in Constantinople as the representative of the larger portion of the Church. Even worse, even in Holy Etchmiadzin a sort of oddness has come about whereby the catholicosal residence has become isolated from the rest of the monastic order. (All who know something of the present situation in Holy Etchmiadzin would agree with us). That, of course, must be regarded as a voluntary abuse that occurred because of individual personalities; it may be corrected in the future, when those personalities give way to others. The basic idea of our Church's high governance will remain the same as it always has: Holy Etchmiadzin, as the head, will have close and immediate links with all of its parts—with all the representatives of the Armenian (Apostolic) clergy—wherever and in whichever country they happen to be.

I do not think it necessary to wash our proverbial dirty linen in public, so I must remain silent. There's plenty of time to talk.

Speaking of national unity, it is impossible not to recall those of our brothers who, through religious differences, have separated from us. I refer to the Armenian Protestants and Armenian Catholics. The press is at present concerned with that subject. But we'd never allow ourselves to be against freedom of conscience if religious divisions did

---

13. The thrones of the Catholicos of All Armenians (in Etchmiadzin, then in Russia) and the Armenian Patriarch of Constantinople.
14. Kevork IV, Catholicos of All Armenians, whose seat was the monastery at Holy Etchmiadzin.

not harm Turkish Armenian national unity and split the whole community. But when we see protestantism become a tool in the hands of the British for various political ends that have nothing to do with Christianity and religion, it is impossible to remain indifferent. Whoever has seen the Protestants in Europe would possibly laugh at our judgement, but Protestants are not the same in Asia. Separating from the mother Church there, they become totally different people. All their links with their nation are severed and they look at their own people in the same way as the Jews once looked at the Samaritans. It is not even necessary to speak of the Catholics; they too are bad. One calls himself "Ingiliz" (English), the other "Frang" (Frank or French). If they behave like this, then Apostolic Armenians are not far behind in their intolerance of their separated brothers, thus giving the latter more opportunity to distance themselves.

Travelling at one time in Turkish Armenia, I've had the opportunity to meet Armenian Protestants and Armenian Catholics. I've been in their schools and meeting-houses and occasionally had heated discussions with them. One must feel sorry for those people; they are very poor. The missionaries have taught them so little: specific parts of the Old and New Testaments, a few prayers and, a little Christian doctrine.[15] Additionally, if we add the belief that whoever is not of their church is deprived of the Christian heaven, we have the sum of their knowledge.

In our opinion, those divisions are only temporary phenomena that will naturally disappear when the idea of nationality, in all its creative power, takes shape among them.

It is very desirable that all important Armenians[16] belong to one church, but when catholicism and protestantism are already established institutions, what can we do? Our churchmen do not possess the spirit to work to reunite them with us, so free competition in the religious sphere must be allowed to continue, while work must be carried on to preserve their union with us in terms of national identity. We are of the opinion that the many forms of religious doctrine will not destroy national unity; unity must be sought, in those harmonious parts, as the basic motive for nationality in its

---

15. The author is referring to the missionaries of all persuasions here.
16. The word used here is 'askayinnere': national people, i.e. those individuals important in Armenian national life.

highest sense. We are convinced that a united but separate church in the same nation may lead the nation to partisanship and therefore towards lifelessness; meanwhile, the opposite scenario—involving divided parts that lack a leading national spirit that expresses everyone's interests—will lead the nation to weakness and destruction.

We repeat: we must let competition continue on its way; with it, the Apostolic Armenians will gain more than if they persecute their brothers. The Turkish Armenians did not gain little from that competition. If printing as well as literature generally began to flourish among them, that was due to the rivalry with Venice.[6] If the Turkish Armenians started to improve and multiply their schools, that was due to their competition with the Protestants. Protestantism is, at present, very active, but one should not expect any supposed danger from them. The missionaries working in Asia Minor belong to the American Methodist Board, which has nothing to do with Anglicans or the British and is, in fact, very much against the latter. If real Anglicans were to mix with Armenians, then the situation would be different; they could be dangerous, as many Armenians would "fall into their laps" to obtain protection from consuls and agents.

If we examine the reason for religious changes in Turkey, we may see that doctrinal belief and conscience are of secondary importance; the majority of those leaving their Church have done so because of various material needs. You can often see it: a missionary appears in a particular place—he chooses an obscure place, where intellectual and material poverty rule. The people who listen to his first sermons are those who act as servants in his house: his cooks, personal attendants, grooms, their wives and so on. Obtaining great means from his homeland and taking advantage of Turkey's low costs, he is able, for very little money, to surround himself with numerous servants and enjoy a good lifestyle. To the list of servants may be added teachers, print workers, special preachers and all those who perform any sort of function—whoever receives a salary from the missionary. His small church is established in this way. But if a servant's salary is cut or he is deprived of his place on the servant list, on the following day he will not appear to hear the "Reverend's" sermon.

Of course, the "Reverend" cannot give all his listeners a job and salary so, to maintain them, he is forced to help them in other ways, either by giving them money, shielding them from this or that form of extortion or enticing them with various promises or hopes. One proof, which I witnessed, may explain how essential such a church may be considered: a villager obtains a loan of a few lira from the missionary and uses it to buy an ox. (They quite often lend money with interest to their listeners to increase the debt). The villager subsequently attends to hear the "Reverend's" sermons, but later ceases to do so. The missionary demands his lira and receives this answer from the crafty villager: "I've already repaid my debt to you. You gave me a few lira, in exchange for which I attended your church for a few months. Now that you want your money back, you'll have to attend our [Apostolic] church for three months so that we may be even." This is more likely to happen, of course, among the more mature people, but the children who receive their education in the missionary schools, are significantly different from their fathers.

Those school pupils are also bribed from the start, and thus learn about money. The poor child, entering the missionary's school, receives books, paper and all that is necessary for his schooling, free of charge. He often receives a uniform and even a special weekly payment. He learns to live at someone else's expense, eventually leaving school a completely changed man. He learns to dress well, eat well, but does not learn anything that will earn him a living. He looks down on his father's occupation with shame and is forced to apply to the missionary for work. The missionary, however, has not got work for everyone. He remains unemployed and without means. He becomes even poorer than his father, and at this point, he is ready to fall into anyone's lap—even to change his religion, if it were to provide him with the means to earn a living. It would be improper to call the purveyors of this scheme anything but "salesmen of religion"; it is from this that the mass of adventurers emerge, fleeing from catholicism to protestantism or vice versa, wherever they are well rewarded. That happens not only to individuals; I know a complete

Protestant community where American missionaries have toiled for more than 40 years and spent millions but, when they began to reduce the sums spent in the community,[17] representatives of that community were sent to London to ask the Anglican bishops to send them parish priests, in the hope that they would be wealthier.

From the above, it is plain that the main reason for the changes of religion in Turkey is to be found in the appalling poverty of the Armenian people, which has been caused by intolerable extortion by the Muslims. How stable a church that is founded on a community's poverty and on taking advantage of its straitened circumstances is readily imagined. When a community's economic situation is reformed and life is protected, it becomes the owner of its material possessions and its fate. I'm convinced that in those new circumstances, those kinds of changes in religion will be automatically prevented and will cease. Such is already the case in those towns where the populace is more or less comfortable, though changes in religion may still occur among the lowest classes suffering under grinding poverty.

I'd be very sad to see a small, exiled community of Armenians in France accept catholicism or, in England, protestantism. I'd be able, like a prophet, to predict that it would disappear in 50 years or a century. I cannot imagine, however, an Armenian turning Catholic or Protestant[18] in Armenia. A small nation, it is true, may be swallowed up and disappear when it joins the church of the governing power—just as all the Armenians who accepted Islam in Turkey were assimilated by the Turks—but it just does not happen when a people in its own homeland accepts another faith that differs from the state religion.

Turkey's myopic government, with the aim of sowing dissension among the Armenians and subverting their unity, has allowed and supported changes of religion among them, but in doing so has fallen

---

17. I believe that the [missionary] Society did not have the right to spend money on any community for more than 30 years. During that period the Society was supposed to complete its work and hand over the costs to the community. The community would then supply financial support for its church. (Author's note)

18. The author uses the terms and "Frang" and "'Ingiliz" here.

from one blunder into a worse one. While Armenians turning Catholic or Protestant did, on the one hand, damage the ties that bound them together, on the other hand such conversions threw the doors open to diplomatic meddling in the affairs of their co-religionists by Catholic and Protestant states (France and England). The ramifications of this mistake are seen in the pages of the Treaty of Berlin. Persia has pursued a wiser policy: it has tried, by all means, to prevent the entry and spread of protestantism and catholicism in the Christian communities within its borders, giving financial assistance to Armenian schools from government funds; they have also sought to improve the rights and importance of the Armenian clergy, so that they can compete with foreign missionaries. Much proof of this is known to me, though I consider its recollection here unnecessary. If Turkey were to reassess its policy and follow Persia's lead, it would gain much by doing so.

However, we have heard, many times, the following thoughts: "What do we lose if the British and French, in changing our religion, begin to sympathise with and protect us? Why should we not take advantage of this situation?" All the Vasags and Meroujans[19] thought this way, but our nation was severely punished for the consequences of this policy. Our Kingdom in Cilicia was sacrificed for this policy when the Armenians, belittling their own strength, thought of joining the Greek Orthodox Church, so that they could receive protection from the Byzantine Empire or the Pope. Our history is filled with such examples that have always had negative results.

We repeat: it is very sad to see a part of the Armenian nation in Turkey separated from the national whole, but as that's an accomplished fact of history, ways must be found to promote unity and not enlarge the difference. The argument is between differences of opinion vis-à-vis how unity is to be achieved. To repeat the cliché of patriotism: we are people of one Church, our nationality is recognised by our Church, whoever is not of the Church of St. Gregory the Illuminator is not Armenian, and so forth; maybe those sermons were once necessary but are now very tired and outdated. It is impossible to make use of those sermons: they are dangerous in as

---

19. Vasag and Meroujan are two historical figures who have been castigated as traitors in popular Armenian historiography.

much as they may present the opportunity to completely distance Protestant and Catholic Armenians from the nationally unified whole. The only way for the Armenians in Turkey to unite is not for the Armenians separated from the Armenian Apostolic Church to return to it, but to spread the idea of nationality among them. Members of a nation may belong to this or that church, but still form a complete body, collecting together all these scattered forces to work against tyranny and extortion. They may together throw off that intolerable yoke carried, with the same burden, by everyone.

Many say that such an approach is impossible in Asia; they say that the Armenian Church may become a rallying point, and that the ideal of nationality would only have an effect in Europe, where each person may even be a non-believer but belong to a nation, and so on. These are very narrow-minded judgements. Whatever route the Europeans have taken to reach that point, you can take the same; civilisation will not deny you those things that belong to humanity. Was not Europe the same several centuries ago as the Armenians are today? Did not the Europeans also get confused between nationality and the church, and have they not now understood that nationality and religion are two different ideals?

Sophistry and rancid patriotism progress hand-in-hand, even in our midst. Some say that Armenian Catholics and Armenian Protestants do not have a history—that only the followers of St. Gregory the Illuminator have, because history belongs to them. A worse, more childish way of thinking cannot be imagined. If our past is only contained in our Church, then why are we proud of the pagans Haik, Aram, Dikran and so forth that came before King Dertad and St. Gregory the Illuminator? So, should we start our history from the day of the foundation of the Armenian Apostolic Church and not consider those who came before as Armenians because they were fire worshippers and did not belong to the Church? But we do not make that distinction with our history. How can we say to the Armenian Catholics or Protestants that they have no history, when they are a continuation of the same race—especially when Haik, Aram, Dikran, Dertad, Gregory the Illuminator, Vartan, Nerses the Great and so on, as much as they belong to the Armenian

Church, belong likewise to the Armenian Protestant and Armenian Catholic Churches? National history, the past of a nation, belongs to the entire nation, regardless of whatever religion or sect its parts belong to.

If today the Armenian Protestants and Armenian Catholics do not consider themselves Armenian, it is due to impoliteness. Does not the impolite Apostolic Armenian look at them in the same way? Does he consider the Protestant and the Catholic as Armenian? As the Catholic calls himself "Frang", so the Apostolic Armenian calls him the same. Such thinking comes from the conviction that nationality must be found in the Church, and it disappears when the ideal of nationality, through education, becomes general throughout the nation's separated parts.

Turkish government officials are well aware of the aforementioned circumstances; "divide and rule" is their motto. As Armenians, every one of us has a contemptuous opinion about the Turks. Although they are not intellectuals and are famous individually as robbers who despoil the palace treasury and leave the inhabitants of entire provinces in total destitution, in terms of cunning, diplomatic deceit and general machiavellism they are extremely talented. They understand the relations that exist between all the races, as well as their aspirations; if they see the smallest sign of danger, they know the necessary or suitable way to stifle those aspirations or completely eradicate them. They are not above exploiting even the most trifling opportunities to sow the seeds of dissension in a race to destroy its cohesion. They have known for a very long time how to demolish Armenian unity, which does not recognise Armenians outside the Armenian Apostolic Church. That is the reason why changes of religion among the populace have occurred so quickly, and the government has provided assistance in this area. Given all of this, it is not surprising to see that alongside the Armenian Question the dead feud between the "Hassounians" and "Anti-Hassounians"[20] has been resurrected.

---

20. An internal dispute between two sections of the Catholic Armenian clergy in Constantinople.

Fostering religious divisions by various means in order to perpetuate disunity among various races and keep them at odds—this is a policy with a long history and one adopted by the Mongol Turks from the Byzantine throne. The Armenians were not their sole target; the same was repeated with the Assyrian Nestorian masses and those separated from Nestorianism, in the Chaldeans, Maronites, Jacobites, Copts and all the Christian races. Who does not know about the shameful disturbances on Easter Day every year in the Church of St. James in Jerusalem, between the Armenian, Latin and Greek priests? Disregarding the continual protests of the Armenian and Greek Patriarchates, the Sublime Porte has never imposed rules or limits upon them, nor has it determined the rights of these parties, despite the fact that doing so would force the priests to stop fighting one another every year.

2

We have digressed from our subject considerably, dwelling for some time on the subject of changes in religion within the populace. Showing that there are no links or communication between the Turkish Armenians and us, and expressing the thought that we are bound to help them may lead the reader to expect that we must demonstrate some kind of new link with them or that we should say how we would do so. None of these things is the subject of our article. We must follow the method of a clever doctor, who first researches the patient's being, studies his entire life, examines his pain and understands its symptoms, and then determines the cure.

At the beginning, we stated that we do not completely know our Turkish Armenian brothers and what they are lacking; their situation and all its aspects are unknown to us. As a result, whatever we write and whatever we think concerning them will be defective, biased and, in many cases, groundless supposition. We must have accurate information, base our thinking on the greater meaning of the problem and understand—as we should—their needs, while studying all the most important aspects of their lives and situation, their economic state, their past and present political situation and so forth. Expressions of brotherhood or empty demonstrations of patriotism are not enough in themselves when they only result in castles in the air and the poor Turkish Armenian having nowhere to lay his head and rest.

There has to be mutual understanding between us. We are still lacking in a legitimate syntax for Turkish Armenia. What light can a few scattered, lightweight, meaningless articles in journals throw on their lives? We need complete demographic[21] information, based on facts—not only to study the lives of Armenians, but also those of the Turks, Kurds, Circassians and other races that presently live in Armenia. We require complete geographical information concerning the population, production, topography, road communications and the natural as well as political life of Armenia. We need accurate statistical and economic information about the Armenian population specifically and non-Armenian races generally. We even need to know the spirit that pervades the different races living in Turkey—their natures, directions, tendencies, and religious and moral feelings—in other words, their complete intellectual and psychological composition.

The Constantinople Armenian press and its literature gave us none of the aforementioned types of information, nor did it want to: it is with this attitude in mind that we must search for the greatest reason behind their lack of success. The literati of Turkey were such uneducated, petty people (although, it must be confessed that there are no great men among us either) that they could not think of what use that information might be to them or what they should write about. The limited intellectual means available locally were not able to create great talents for great works and, remaining weak, were not able to serve the greatest national demand: salvation from heavy foreign influence. Although there are no great talents among us, there are educated people who are able to work in a better andd more practical way than the people of Constantinople.

But there are some people who think thus: "Leave the Turkish Armenians alone and do not raise questions in their minds; they know better thann us what they must do… We have great hopes for

---

21. The author has used the Armenian word for 'demographic' (concerning social statistics) here, then immediately followed it with the transliteration of the word 'ethnographic' (concerning the classification of various cultural and racial groups) in brackets.

them..." and so on. It is possible to write entire books with words of this sort, if only there was a wish to string meaningless, empty words together. If only we knew what those hopes were based on! The surprise is that these senile sophists dare to predict a "wonderful" future, bereft of hope for a completely downtrodden people, without knowing them or understanding their current situation. They resemble those keening old women who are called to cry over corpses: it is all the same to them, regardless of who and what sort of person the deceased was. They may not even have known him—he may even have been a complete nonentity—but they always sing their usual dirge, lauding the wonderful deeds he never did and his virtues, moving people to sadness and pity, because they have been paid to do so.

There is always "hope"—that is the word of the sophists, although empty hope without action does not achieve anything. Those proponents of inertia, I believe, want an unchanging humanity comprised of innocents; it is immaterial that there's life in them.

No, we must speak; we must think of our Turkish Armenian brothers. We must examine them, and in the most critical way. However, as we have not studied them thoroughly, and as we have not got (or tried to get) accurate and detailed information about their state, all our efforts and work in helping them will be fruitless. To remain distant, not to enter into work, not to know the real demands of a nation and to only create idealistic delusions—all this is charming, but false. These illusions self-destruct when they collide with reality.

We repeat: until today, there has never been nor is there any powerful link between us and our Turkish Armenian brothers. We have explained the reasons. There will be a mutual link between us when there is an exchange of thought—an exchange which the press and literature really must serve. Literary correspondence would have the positive effect of creating a general standardised literary language. This is most important, as there are many dialects. Although on the one hand they demonstrate the richness of the language, on the other they dilute and isolate the monumental strength of our literary teaching and create difficulties in national relations within the same race.

Our Turkish Armenian brothers are bereft of help, because they are both uneducated and poor. The combined lack of education and poverty create great difficulties in a nation's progress, and such is the case with Turkish Armenians. It is every Armenian's duty to help them, with the greatest duty resting with the Russian Armenians. We pay little significance to the specific gifts that are given in the name of this or that society in Turkey, as we do not know how appropriate those organisations are; nevertheless, we cannot dismiss our people's praiseworthy efforts in trying to at least assist our needy brothers.

It hurts to admit that the assistance given to our Turkish Armenian brothers—which our people gave and continue to provide—is so insignificant that it must be considered totally insufficient and unworthy of even being mentioned. The rich people among us have very seldom joined those efforts. That section of the people, in whose heart all national feelings have frozen—and for whose amusement and glory they waste great sums of money—have, with singular exceptions, given nothing for the needy in Turkey. Our clergy, those ecclesiastics who have thought only of their own interests and purses, remained completely indifferent; in terms of policy, they have remained silent when the Armenian Question has been raised, stubbornly remaining cold-hearted and uncharitable in giving material assistance. Our aristocratic and so-called *chinovnik* (official) public was no less stony-hearted than a wealthy and oppressive merchant or the clergy who stifle all good intentions. One thing that is striking and comforting is that the groaning of our needy brothers in Turkey was recognised by our lower classes—the poor peasant, the journeyman worker, the retailers in small towns and the always penniless student who, from their slender resources, kept aside a small amount for their brothers who were in greater need.

Where did this hard-heartedness towards our brothers of the same blood come from, and how did we become so unfeeling? As stated in the first part of this article, we recognise but one reason: that there has never been a close link between the Armenians of Turkey and us. We were separated from one another and, in that state, our national cohesiveness has deteriorated to such an extent that we have become almost completely foreign to each other. The latest Russo-Turkish war broke out and we read and heard about the bitter poverty of our poor brothers. Some hearts were found among us that had not quite turned to stone and were moved to pity. They became enthusiastic and thought of extending a helping hand. But because that enthusiasm was momentary and the result of a temporary situation, it did not become permanent, did not become fundamental, but instead disappeared when the reason behind the enthusiasm vanished. This is what happened and was to happen. At first we very often read in *Mshag* the lists of donors to the "Araratian Society";[22] now the lists are growing smaller and, soon, they may disappear altogether.

Retaining the enthusiasm of a people for a good cause requires energetic means and spirited work—not only to persuade the people to contribute materially to the cause, but mainly to make them understand that they are performing a supreme duty. Several times the idea has been published in *Mshag* that we ought to form a committee that would concern itself with collecting money, with the aim of providing it to newly-opened local schools and to aid in the general spread of education. With a complete appreciation for the said idea, and turning once more to the aforementioned considerations, we should gather basic information and accurately research the situation and needs of our brothers in Turkey—adding that the aim of such a committee would be very limited, were it to focus merely on material aid. This is because, before providing assistance, it is important to understand their greatest needs, their immediate demands, in a word, their problems, which need swift cure. All of this is impossible without being completely acquainted with their state. But such information about them is very sparse.

Some may remark that it is not our business to collect such information; we collect money, we hand it to them and they know their own requirements very well—let them use the funds provided for whatever institution they please. We would be remiss if we implied the idea that we should interfere in their organisations or, in giving them funds, make ourselves their directors. Such ideas are far from our intent. Nonetheless, we cannot hide our suspicion that the active part of the Turkish Armenian community has studied the needs of the people in-depth, as is required. It is impossible to restore a fallen nation with reading, writing and the alphabet alone; doing so requires other means that should advance in tandem with education. (We do not want to mention the fact that our Turkish Armenian agents are used to making a great deal of noise, through childish

---

22. An Armenian charitable organization founded in Constantinople in 1876 to aid Armenians in the Ottoman Empire and the Caucasus.

enthusiasm, even when they only carry out some small or even trifling work).

In our opinion, this fundamental task must be started; to that end, instead of scattering resources on specific aims, we must collect them, centralise them into a complete entity and use them in a collective manner. It could not have been done in any other way when a committee was formed of Russian Armenians, mainly to assist in charitable efforts to ameliorate the needs of our brothers in Turkey. That committee would have been able to gather all the information needed about Turkey mentioned above. It could have sent intelligent travellers to study the state of the Armenians in Turkey and publish their findings—not only in Armenian, but in many languages. It could have, by now, collected all the pieces of information available, compiled them and published the results in separate books and translations. It seems obvious that a committee like this, apart from providing material and moral assistance, would have been able to provide so much more help, that we feel it unnecessary to mention. It would have been enough to acquaint not only us Russian Armenians, but the whole of the educated world with the state of Turkish Armenia. Then we'd definitely know what they needed and in what ways we could help.[23]

The state of nations is never suddenly transformed, nor is it ever improved from one day to the next; preparation for it begins maybe several centuries beforehand and, at the right time, it is put into practice. The Turkish Armenians were not prepared to take great advantage of the times and, due to this, could not reach their goals— although some look at paragraph 61 of the Treaty of Berlin[24] and see a goldmine. We are not much dazzled by that mine. This or that

---

23. We heard, a long time ago, that a wealthy Russian Armenian had the wish to establish a high school in Turkish Armenia and to that end was having teachers trained. If that is true, for when in the future is he keeping the school and teachers? (Author's note)

24. Article 61 of the Treaty of Berlin reads: "The Sublime Porte undertakes to carry out, without further delay, the improvements and reforms demanded by local requirements in the provinces inhabited by Armenians, and to guarantee their security against the Circassians and Kurds. It will periodically make known the steps taken to this effect to the powers, who will superintend their application."

paragraph, especially if it is inserted for appearance's sake, has as much significance in the rebirth of a nation as a prescription for a patient who cannot use medication.

We recognise but one mine from which the hoped-for gold can possibly be obtained, if mined constantly and unceasingly—it is called preparation. The question of the Turkish Armenians from this point on turns on ceaseless and uninterrupted preparation, in order that they stand organised and ready for that great day when the bell of freedom's hour is sounded again. That day will come again, and yet again... It is perhaps not so far off...

Many people discontentedly say "The Eastern Question will not come to a conclusion this time, either," or "Oh! When will that Eastern Question end?" These are very naïve statements. The Eastern Question is of vital importance to Europe. The problems of life do not simply end; they only become temporarily conditioned. In the entire Armenian nation I know of only one man who really understands what the Eastern Question means, and who understood that diplomatic term when it was unknown to most of us. Can the Eastern Question end? No; it will be there for as long as the east exists. It is a historic problem and will always be in the history of nations. At one time, eastern nations invaded Europe like a flood, to pillage it. Now the roles have changed; Europe is invading the east to take advantage of Asia's riches. Every wave of invasion generates a new Eastern Question and at this time, the Russians and the British have interests in the east and are competing with one another. The Germans, the French and the others will then start. With growth, each European state is being squeezed within its own narrow borders and using up its own riches; they must look to the east to find necessary resources. Each new offensive or act of colonisation creates a new Eastern Question. If the European movement to the east has been slow up until now, that is thanks to the United States, whose appearance weakened their drive to Asia for a few centuries. Now America has started to fill up too. So the Eastern Question exists (and will continue to exist); the Turkish Armenians must make preparations to take advantage of favourable events, when they occur.

And if the Turkish Armenians remain unready?

Then unfortunate Armenia—that historic bridge between Europe and Asia—will be crushed and disappear under the movement of other nations.

REPORT[25]

Oppressions in the Provinces, Constantinople, 1876
(Official publications of the Armenian National Patriarchate)

In the last few months of last year,[26] a booklet was published with the above title; it contained details of the oppression[27] carried out among the Armenian population of the Asiatic provinces [of the Ottoman Empire]. It was an official publication produced from the records of the Armenian Patriarchate of Constantinople and presented to the National Assembly there in September 1876.

The curtain was raised and we now know what is happening on the stage.

Until today, we have had very little information about the Patriarchate in Constantinople—or, in other words, about the workings of the National Constitution.[28] Until today we have had practically no idea what significance the Armenian National Assembly of Constantinople has had with the Sublime Porte and to

---

25. "Deghegakirk", *Mshak*, 1877.
26. The year is not specified in the text but the date of this work, based on internal evidence, is probably 1878/9.
27. The word used here is 'haresdaharoutiune, which has several meanings, the chief of which are oppression, extortion, violence and depredation. I have used one or another of these translations according to context.
28. Raffi is referring here to the Armenian National Constitution, which was promulgated in 1864 by an Ottoman Imperial decree. This constitution or set of regulations were meant for the orderly administration of the internal affairs of the Apostolic Armenian Community (more popularly known as the Armenian *millet*).

what extent it has been able to aid the people in the provinces outside Constantinople. The "Report" cited above offers some interesting but very sad information.

The "Report" is divided into two parts. The first contains the collected records of the oppressions carried out in the provinces during the last 20 years and is entitled "A: Report on the Oppression Carried Out in the Provinces [addressed to] the Sublime Porte by the [Armenian] National Assembly on 11 April 1872". The Report has a seal and signature: "Archbishop Megerditch Khrimian, Patriarch of Constantinople".[29]

The subjects covered in the aforementioned Report, as we said, were created from the 20-year records held by the Patriarchate; they stretch to April 11, 1872. The second Report has the title "Second Report on the Oppression in the Provinces from the Committee of the Council [addressed to] the National Assembly"; it contains the records of oppression in the provinces from 1872 until September 1, 1876—in other words, the records of oppression for the whole five-year span. It means that the entire two-part Report represents the work of the Patriarchate for the whole 25-year period. It is not known how many protests were received from the provinces by the Patriarchate during that time; the only thing that's known is that the Patriarchate was in official communication or negotiation with the Sublime Porte concerning 57 different matters. That is a very small number, bearing in mind the many injustices that were perpetrated in the Asian provinces during those 25 years.

To give the reader some small idea of the oppression carried out in Asiatic Turkey, we consider it necessary to introduce the contents of both the first and second Reports.

The first contained the following subjects:

1. In the matter of enforcing the law and justice, the provincial authorities are generally careless and indifferent. As a result of their whims, they abuse, in accordance with their pleasure, the highest written commands aimed at reducing oppression and punishing those who practise it.

---

29. Later elected His Holiness Megerditch I, Supreme Patriarch and Catholicos of All Armenians—also known with great affection as Khrimian Hairig (little father).

2. As the provincial government meetings are organised in accordance with the Teshkilat law,[30] they are monopolised by venal people.

3. The provincial Armenian, being subject to the fanaticism of the Muslims, always becomes the subject of hostile insults and dishonour.

4. Armenians have to work without pay on the construction of royal edifices; whoever cannot do so is subject to unjust monetary demands.

5. Armenians also have to work without pay on road construction or, for this reason, are harassed to do so.

6. Taxation officials, instead of taking 10 percent of a crop, demand real silver in its place.

7. In the same way, 10 percent of the crop grown in a garden to feed a family is taken by force.

8. The peasant is forced to move that 10 percent of the crop to the tax official's storehouse.

9. Because the tax official deliberately arrives late, the crop rots (having been left in the fields in the rain because the peasant does not have the right to harvest it before the 10-percent tax has been collected). In such a case, instead of taking 10 percent of the rotten crop, the official demands 10 percent of a good crop, in silver.

10. The peasant is forced to provide free hospitality and food in his own home for the tax official and his aides.

11. The tax officials, calculating what has to be given by counting the number of yokes available for oxen, takes illegal and excessive amounts of wheat from the peasant.

12. Apart from the extortion practised by tax officials (as shown above), they force provincial Armenians to pay the forbidden shahanalik and olchuk-hakke taxes.[31]

13. The people left alive after such extortion are forced to pay the military taxes for those who have died, emigrated or escaped.[32]

14. Due to the continuous distribution and redistribution of land and political taxes, the burden that should fall on the Muslims is actually borne by the Armenians.

---

30. A form of court that is composed of Moslems and non-Moslems and is called a *Teshkilat*, where non-Moslems are elected or appointed for appearances' sake. (Author's note)

15. Due to the payment of taxes, penniless people are forced to sell essential home furnishings, agricultural tools and even animals, and they are are beaten by the police and suffer the severity of being jailed.

16. Women and grown children are forced to accept the Muslim religion

17. Due to the non-acceptance of the testimony of non- Muslims in courts, the rapes, robberies and killings that Armenians suffer remain unpunished.

18. Under the extortions and robberies by armed Kurds, mountain tribes, Circassians and Turkish derebegs, the Armenian people are oppressed and suffering.

19. Women, brides and virgins are being kidnapped and raped.

---

31. The main extortionists are tax officials. Provincial officials give the majority of the 10% tax on the crop to a relative or friend with interest and secretly become partners with them. If, when the crop is sold, it receives a good price, the tax official receives the 10% with profit. When the crop has no value, considering it to be expensive, he demands tax payment in money, which in any event he has no right to keep. But the peasant is forced to accept the tax official's tyranny because, if he protests, the official leaves his fields, allowing the crops to go rotten under rain and snow. Then, the tax official has the right to claim double the 10% value in silver, because the crop has rotted. The local government tolerates the official's tyranny because it is a partner in the profits.

Olchuk-hakke means the cost for measuring. *Shahanalik*: means royal. (Author's note)

32. In Turkey, because the Armenians don't provide soldiers, they pay a tax named *bedel* ('in place of'). This tax has to be collected in the following manner: on the basis of one soldier for every 180 men, in place of the soldier 5,000 kurush (300 rubles) has to be paid. Those who are under 15 and over 75 years of age, as well as members of the clergy, the poor and those who are without means are supposed to be free from paying. But the government officials, disregarding those exceptions, and only utilizing their own whims, take as much as they can from the people. Leaving that aside, the Mohammedan, who provides soldiers, has special privileges and rights. But the Armenian, who pays in silver instead of providing soldiers, has no such rights or privileges. Bearing in mind the enormous number of emigrants from Asiatic Turkey, it's possible to understand how heavy the burden of military taxes is on the remaining people, because it is collected on the basis of the national population. (Author's note)

These are the items covered in the first Report which, until 1872—a whole 20 years—were the subjects being dealt with by official negotiations between the Patriarchate and the Sublime Porte. But what has the Porte done to stop the oppression?

We would like to address the following point made by the committee to the National Assembly, regarding the Patriarchate's records:

> From the date of the Report's presentation (April 11, 1872), it would appear from the data collected by the committee that the written protests (*takrirs*) made by the Patriarchate about depredation are being left without result, being scrapped, or left without reply. They are being left to the fruitless *istilam*[33] system, making the orders sent by the central government to the provinces unworkable; these protests are forgotten, and the local population is given no recourse whatsoever.

The point made by the committee may be translated into our language in this way. From 1852 to 1872, the Patriarchate received many different types of protest from the provinces about oppressions taking place and, with its written protests in hand, addressed the Sublime Porte to request satisfaction. The Porte either hid the protests, left them without any result, did not think them worthy of answers or, if they were accepted, promulgated orders that were put aside by provincial officials. In this way, the Armenian people remained in wretchedness… and none of the Patriarchate's protests achieved their aims.

During the present crisis in Turkey, many people have been interested as to whether this state has progressed or not in the last 20 years, or whether its government has improved the situation of its Christian subjects. People who have been hiding Turkish barbarities

---

33. The Sublime Porte would often return a written protest from a particular province or county concerning exactions (or oppressions) for clarification or re-examination. This was a cunning method of deceiving the protestor, as the provincial authorities would never want to justify the protester's statements, as quite often they were involved in the depredations that were the subject of the protest in the first place. The *istilam* was something similar. It was a method of dragging out the time taken to examine the problem, leading to its being forgotten. (Author's note)

and have trumpeted Turkey's imaginary progress—and who have been blinded by their own personal interests—have declared that Turkey has significantly reformed, the state of Christian subjects is relatively much improved, they now enjoy almost complete freedom and so on.

All these statements are nothing but empty words.

Turkey has only advanced in one thing: presenting itself externally as a European country, while in its heart, soul and activities it has always remained Mongolian, with the same nature as it had in the deserts of Turan.

Studying the 25-year records in the "Report", we are even more certain that the state of the Turkish government in the past is still seen today, while the state of the non-Muslim population, instead of improving, has got worse.

To make this truth plainer, we refer the reader to the "Second Report", which contains the records of the oppression carried out during the five-year period from 1872 until today. What do we see there?

The majority of the items in the "Second Report" relate to occurrences of oppression, indicating that injustices have gradually increased.[34] The different methods of oppression have increased and the criminality of the oppressors is more terrifying. Two things remain unchanged: one, the government's weak methods and unsatisfactory results and two, the places where oppression takes place,[35] as the same injustices continue to happen in the same way and in the same places. Why?

---

34. The first report covers a 20-year period and only contains 19 items, while the second covers five years and has 38 items. Apart from this, new kinds of items appear in the second report that don't appear in the first. These relate to 284 villages and lands belonging to monasteries forcibly taken over by Mohammedans. It also mustn't be forgotten that the second report concerns things happening in the most recent times. (Author's note)

35. In both the first and second reports the centres of oppression are the provinces on all four sides of Lake Van, in other words those of Erzerum and Dikranagerd (Diarbekir) as well as the counties of Moush, Paghesh, Van, Terchan, Kghi, Ghoughoulchan, Charsanjak, Seghert, Sasoun and others. (Author's note)

The reason is very simple. It is with this that an answer is given to the question of how far Turkey has progressed in 25 years: yes, there have been great advances—in the new ways in which the non-Muslim nations are harassed, robbed and dishonoured. So that the reader may be convinced of the truth of this statement, we have inserted the subjects of the Patriarchate's "Second Report" here, whose contents are written more clearly and in greater detail.[36]

Oppressions

1. Against the oppression of the tyrant Shah-Hussein, the kaymakam of Ghoughoulchan in the county of Yerzinga (Erzinjan), in the provincial governorship of Erzerum. From the beginning of the Patriarchate of Archbishop Megerditch Khrimian (from 1873) until today, there have been an unceasing number of protests addressed to the Sublime Porte. The Porte has instituted "decisive" measures to have the villain dismissed from his post and the peace of the people respected. The Grand Vizier, as well as the Minister of the Interior, the Minister of Foreign Affairs and others, have promulgated five magnificent decrees and sent them to the governor of Erzerum. The language used in the decrees is quite strong and persuasive; they tell him, for example, that as "the killer of his father, mother and wife", Shah-Hussein should be dismissed from his post and exiled from the county of Erzinjan. The protests say that as "the killer of hundreds" and the "leader of the Kurdish robbers" and the "harasser of the Christians", Shah-Hussein should be exiled from Erzinjan and, like his father who was exiled for his tyranny, he too should be made to disappear.

The complete text of all five decrees is published in the Report, and their contents, it is true, are persuasive and humanitarian, like all the written, (but unimplemented) supreme decrees that the Sublime Porte produces so lavishly in its factory of deceit.

---

36. Among the subjects raised recently by the Patriarchate with the satrezam (Grand Vizier), which attempted to beg for redress for the Turkish Armenian people, was the name of the villain Shah-Hussein. It seems that the extortions carried out by one man were as important as, for example, that of the question of Armenian property generally, or of making young children change their religion… (Author's note)

Among the seals affixed to the decrees are those of the greatest men in Turkey: Ali, Mahmoud-Nekim, Midhat, Mohammed Rushti, and Hussein Avni. These five have risen from a position of ordinary vizier to a level higher than that of Grand Vizier. But what did the five ministers' decrees achieve? Nothing! By crossing the Constantinople Narrows to Asia Minor, they lost their importance, and the villain Shah-Hussein continues his robberies to this day, because he is protected by another, greater robber—the pasha governor of Erzerum.

From this account, it is understandable why the highest decrees are very often rendered unworkable by local officials.

2. The Kurdish begs (chieftains) of the small town of Sasoun in Seghert (Siirt) county, having forcibly collected government taxes from the Armenians, did not then pass the money on to the treasury. The government, sending troops, recovered the silver from the Kurds, but as soon as the soldiers left, the Kurds once again forcibly collected the same amount of money from the Armenians as they had previously handed over. So that this injustice would not happen again in the future, the government took the decision to build and maintain a barracks with a garrison there, but no action has yet been taken.

3. The oppressor from Moush named Farigh, one of the Kurdish begs, was exiled with his brother, to Kastamouni, by government decree. It is not known by what means he gained his freedom; he returned and vengefully began to torture and rob Armenians. A protest note was once again tendered, and once again cries of protest arose. It all was either left unresolved or dragged out until it was forgotten.

4. A protest note was written by the Patriarchate about the Kurdish oppressors of Pernashen, Khout, Sasoun, Shadakh and in the province of Moush—again, without result.

5. The functionaries in charge of building roads to Maden in Kharpert (Harput) province, using Armenian peasants as forced labour, withheld their daily wages. Protests were raised, but the result (if any) is unknown.

6. Although by government decree the military taxes imposed on the Armenians of the town of Severeg in Dikranagerd (Diarbekir) province have been reduced by one-quarter, the decree has not been implemented; as a result, the whole amount has been collected. Apart

from this, the taxes for those who have died or disappeared are demanded from the rest of the community. In addition, the government officials, putting an inflated value on the land, are burdening the people with exorbitant land taxes. They are also forcing the people to work at building roads for more days than is permitted by law. Again, protests have been made, but the results thereof are unknown.

7. The Armenian monastery of The Souls, near Van, has been looted by the Kurds; everything has been taken. The Patriarchate protested this, but the protest has remained unanswered.

8. The Armenian villages in the Modgan region in the province of Moush have been continually robbed by the Kurds: one year's losses included: 799 sheep, 53,850 keroush in coin (3,167 rubles), 1,972 batmans of foodstuffs and cereals, 121 pieces of clothing and 261 rolls of red canvas. A protest note citing this list has been written and presented to the central government, but there has been no result.

9. A tyrant named Mahmed-Beg, with his twelve sons and relatives, are conducting every kind of oppression in 32 villages in the county of Paghesh (Bitlis). Local Armenian protests have been answered by indifference on the part of the local government; the local Muslim population joined the Armenians and a special protest note was sent to the Armenian Patriarchate in Constantinople. A high-level government decree was promulgated, but its results are not known.

10. Every year the Kurds from Sasoun forcibly take as tax, from the Aghpiurig monastery near Moush, 400 keroush in coin, four cows, 20 sheep, four batmans of tobacco, four batmans of oil and five bushels of wheat. If the monastery does not pay this tax, the monks' lives are put into constant danger. A protest note was written and the Sublime Porte sent a decree, but there have been no known results.

11. Several independent derebegs (chieftains) in the province of Dikranagerd (Diarbekir) are perpetrating dreadful forms of oppression. The central government, in accordance with the protests of the people and the Patriarchate, sent a special inspector. Having established the derebegs' guilt, they were brought to Dikranagerd and a decision was made for them to permanently remain in the city. But as soon as the government inspector departed, the derebegs returned to their homes and resumed their crimes with increased violence. More protests were subsequently made, but the criminals have always remained unpunished.

12. Because there were popular protests against the deputy governor of Marash, Sayid Pasha, and on the basis of a written protest from the Patriarchate, the central government sent a decree for the local government to examine the situation. But the local government not only didn't do so, but tried to show that the Armenians were falsely accusing Sayid Pasha. He had a statement prepared to that effect and had even forced the local clergyman, who was the deputy to the prelate of the diocese, to sign it to prove that Sayid Pasha was innocent. A protest was sent to the Patriarchate against this violence, but the result of that protest is unknown.

13. The Armenians of the town of Ak-Shehir are burdened with impossible sums to pay, as the usual taxes levied on them have been set at a higher level. The Patriarchate has written a protest note, which has remained without reply.

14. The Patriarchate has sent a written protest note about the losses the Armenians of the Kars region have suffered as a result of extortion at the hands of Kurds and Kurdish begs from Maden. The Patriarchate has sent a protest note that has remained unanswered.

15. A protest note was written about the injustices perpetrated by police Major Dilaver Agha and his relatives in the Van area. It has remained unanswered.

16. The irregular distribution of military taxes and the extra amount that the Armenians have to pay was the subject of a protest note, but the result is not known.

17. The Armenians of the village of Sarmousakli, in the province of Sepastia (Sivas), have been oppressed by Muslims. Their cruelty reached such a pitch that they took an Armenian woman by force up the mountain and, after satisfying their lust, killed her and threw her body in the river. A protest note was written and the Sublime Porte issued orders, but the result is unknown.

18. The Nayib-Effendi of the civil court in Ourfa (Urfa) refuses to accept Christian witnesses, in breach of the laws of the courts. This was the subject of a protest note of which there has been no known result.

Agrarian or Land Matters

[19.] A Muslim woman, having unjustly taken ownership of the whole of the land belonging to the Armenian village of Sati in Dikranagerd (Diarbekir), considers herself their landlord, and so has forced the villagers to give her a portion of their crops. Several protest notes have been written; some have remained unanswered, while the others have garnered no result.

20. A Muslim priest (*mufti*) has forcibly taken over the land of the village of Monrig, in the province of Moush (Mush). At the same time, the governor of Erzerum personally arrived in the area, and because Moush was within his jurisdiction, he listened to the villagers' protests, found the mufti's forced take-over illegal, and gave the peasants new land ownership documents. In this way, the peasants once more became the owners of the land they had tilled for 40-50 years. But when the governor of Erzerum changed, the land arrangements also changed. The mufti, having had a few of the peasants brought to the city of Moush, obtained, in the local council meeting (by way of threats and force), testimony that the land belonged to the mufti and not to the villagers. In this way, he became the owner of the land. The villagers then began to protest that two peasants couldn't be considered representatives of an entire village, that they had no right to say anything on behalf of the all the peasants and so on. But the mufti, being an influential person, prevented their protest from being heard locally. The poor people sent two representatives on their behalf to Constantinople, giving them their land ownership documents and other written evidence. In Constantinople the matter was again examined, but the decision was made in favour of the mufti. The Patriarchate once more wrote a protest note, but the result of it is not known.

21. All the Armenian houses, shops, gardens and vineyards of all the villages in the county of Charsanjak in the province of Kharpert (Harput) were forcibly taken over by a person named Isag-Beg and a number of Muslim aghas (notables) who, as their landlord, imposed payment on the peasants. On the basis of the protests of the villagers and a protest note from the Patriarchate, the central government dispatched a special committee to the county of Charsanjak, to examine the matter. They found the peasants' protest justified and determined that Isag-Beg and the others did not have the right; they sent their findings to the local government to prevent the intervention of the aghas, to recognise the peasants as the owners of the properties and reaffirm the land documents. But that imperial decree has remained unused by the local government, and so Isag-Beg and the other Muslim tyrants remained the owners of the villages in

Charsanjak by various underhand methods. Several more protest notes have been issued, all without results.

22. The local mudir (county governor) of Sepastia (Sivas) settled Circassians on the land and in the fields owned by the Armenians of the village of Yar-Hissar, and thus deprived the villagers of them. The Patriarchate has sent notes of protest several times, but the Sublime Porte has not taken any action.

23. The Muslims of Eski-Shehir have forbidden Christians to buy new areas of land, create settlements or build a church. Protest notes have been written and the Sublime Porte has sent orders several times with the aim of assisting the Christians, but there have been no known results.

24. One of the leaders of the Kurds who carried out oppressive acts in the villages around the town of Espager, in the province of Dikranagerd (Diarbekir), was Abti-Beg; he became the mudir, and has begun to harass the people in every way possible. This tyrant steals the Armenians' fields, land and animals and, appropriating the cemetery of the village of Housp, has demolished the church in it and built himself a house in its place. In a similar way, several other Kurdish begs (whose names are written down) are using oppression in the villages of the town of Eroun. Protest notes have been written and orders have been sent, but the results of them are not known.

25. The Kurdish begs of the Shadakh county of Van have resumed carrying out barbarities, just as they did during times of anarchy in the past. They are torturing the Armenians dreadfully, forcing them to pay taxes to them, destroying their churches, carrying out defilements, burning crops and killing many notable Armenians (whose names are written down). Apart from this, the Armenian inhabitants of six villages in the county of Shadakh (whose names are also written down) have been driven from their homes by Kurds who have settled in their homes and appropriated all their land. All this aside, the land of 12 other villages has been stolen from the Armenians by the Kurds. The local authorities, having received protests from the Armenians, sent Agha-Beg and Megerditch Parseghian to investigate. The investigators, having established the illegality of the Kurds' acts, re-iterated the rights of the Armenians to their lands; the following year, however, a person named Rashid Effendi, being sent to the Shadakh area to put into practice the *tapou* law, secretly transferred those same lands that belonged to the

Armenians to the Kurdish begs as tapou land.[37] As many as 200 peasants took their protest to the local authority in the city of Van, while the Patriarchate, in its turn, sent a protest with the details to the Sublime Porte. That protest has yet to produce any response.

26. The government, regarding the lands belonging to the monastery of Chenkoush as *mahloul*,[38] had them sold. A protest note was written, but the result of it is not known.

During the process of land registration, when it came time to register that which belonged to Armenian national schools and churches, the officials refused to register them as such, saying that they had no instructions to do so; they said, rather, that they had the duty to find their living owners and, when they had checked the rights to a property, to register it in the owners' names. If a property had no living owner, it was to be regarded as mahloul. A protest note was written and the Sublime Porte sent a telegram stating that the land in question should be registered as (Armenian) national property, but there has been no known result.

28. A person named Ali Effendi wants to commandeer a part of the land belonging to the monastery of the Holy Redeemer in Trebizond (Trabzon). A protest note has been written, but no answer has been received.

29. The Muslim residents of the village of Chermoug near the town of Maden are preventing a church from being built in the Armenian quarter, citing the existence of a mosque near the

---

37. The Turkish government sells for a set sum uncultivated land—or rather mortgages it, through its officials—to the peasants and gives them a receipt for the transfer. That is known as tapou. But the only lands that can be considered to be tapou are those without owners and which have not been cultivated. (Author's note)

38. The Turkish government doesn't recognise land as belonging to monasteries or churches, as the owner can only be a recognised person. According to it, a monastery or church is not a living person, so cannot be a landowner... For this reason monastery lands are considered to be mahloul, in other words without an owner. So the government becomes the owner.

Once more it's the same as for monastic land. The laws concerning land are not very well known to us (if there are such laws) but we can't understand why a Muslim mosque and school can have property, but Armenian monasteries and schools can't. (Author's note)

Armenian quarter as the reason. A protest note was written, and a decree was sent, but results for either have not come about.

Murders

30. A telegraph official of Armenian nationality named Asadour was killed in the telegraph office in Aleppo. The government demanded that the telegraph office overseer hand over the criminal. The overseer, pointing out a lowly servant of the telegraph office by the name of Ahmad, said that he was the killer. The local government, without any examination, then said that the apparent killer was "mad" and sent him to a hospital. A protest note was written and a decree was sent, but there are no known results for either.

31. During the Kurds' robbery of the Narek monastery's watermill, the miller was killed. A protest note was written, but no reply has been received.

32. Sergeant Major Hassan, entering the monastery of Aghtamar, killed a member of the monastic order, the priest Hagop. A few Kurds killed the married priest, Reverend Hovhannes, of the village of Mintan. The mass killer Abdul Fattah has threatened to kill all the Armenians within the same area. A protest note was written and a decree and telegram were dispatched by the Sublime Porte, but the results of them (if any) are unknown.

33. Haroutiun Menzerian and Ghazaros Chamchigian were killed by local Muslims in Marash. The local governor of Zeitun, Davoud Agha, had an Armenian policeman by the name of Haroutiun killed. A protest note was written and a telegram was dispatched by the Sublime Porte, but the results thereof are unknown.

34. A protest note was written to the Sublime Porte about the violently anti-Armenian conduct of Mustafa Beg of Malatia, as well as of the activities of hooligans in the town who hung a cross around the neck of a dog and paraded it through the streets and markets. No reply has been received.

Religious Conversions

35. A Turk by the name of Safar kidnapped a girl named Martha from the village of Roumeli, near Baiburt. As a result of Armenian protests, the girl was brought before the local government court for questioning. The Armenian notables of Baiburt, a few Greeks and

some Muslim soldiers were present. Before the girl could answer whether she had willingly converted to Islam, a fanatical mob of Muslims forced their way into the court and began to shout: "The girl has already accepted Islam, there's no need to ask again. If she says that she's not, and returns to Christianity, under sharia law she should have her head cut off." With the angry mob making this and many other similar threats and preventing Martha's mother from approaching her, they forced poor Martha to say that she willingly accepted Islam and forcibly married her to the Turk Safar.

But Martha, not being able to live with a Muslim, escaped to her home by night. This was enough to infuriate the town's Muslims to a fever pitch. The mullahs in the town brought out the drummers[39] and, when all the people had gathered in the Muslim religious schools, they whipped them into a frenzy, saying that the Christians had stolen away the girl who had accepted Islam. About 2,000 enraged armed men immediately attacked Armenian houses and shops; most of them were looted and destroyed and about 30 Armenians were very seriously wounded. The local authorities immediately telegraphed the governor of Garin (Erzerum) about the danger. The governor, arriving there with troops, stopped the violence and, upon hearing that the girl had not been taken away by Christians, took a few men to Erzerum and had them imprisoned. The main troublemakers, however, remained unpunished and no reparations were made to the robbed people. Several protest notes about this were sent to the Sublime Porte, but no reply has been received.

36. In Sepastia (Sivas) an Armenian became a Muslim and took his daughter with him. But because the girl was of adult age, she ran away from her father and took refuge in the Armenian monastery. The Muslims, insisting that she must stay with her father, attacked the monastery and dragged her out by force. The Patriarchate unceasingly wrote protest notes stating that she should be handed over to her Christian mother, as she did not want to take her father's religion. The Sublime Porte wrote an order that she should first live with her Turkified[40] father and an examination should then take

---

39. The word used here is *munedik*. Munediks were drummers used to disseminate news and make announcements to the local populace. They would be akin to town criers in western Europe.

place. The Patriarchate repeated its protest notes. Finally, after three years, they handed her over to her Christian mother for examination, but by that time she had completely changed.

The 37th item concerned the prominent criminal Shah Hussein of Kghi and Yerzenga (Erzinjan), of whom we have already spoken. Much has been written about this criminal in the Report.

The 38th item concerned the military tax, about which we gave a certain amount of information.

The 39th item was about land problems; about this we must speak separately, as this is the greatest question raised in the Report, but it has been paid very little attention by the Patriarchate.

As we have seen, from the contents of both the first and second Reports, if we were to group them by type, we'd obtain the following statistics: of all the 58 items, 36 were concerned with various kinds of oppression, 12 were about land and agricultural problems, five about crimes or criminal offences, and four about religious conversions or the abuse of women. Omitted from the above figures are matters relating to the appropriation by Kurds and Turks of the land belonging to 263 Armenian villages and 21 Armenian monasteries, about which only one general protest note appears to have been sent to the Sublime Porte by the Patriarchate. The land question, which is a vital one for Armenians, has not received much attention, as if it does not interest the Patriarchate.

In any case, let's discuss the 58 items. The Patriarchate has continually sent protest notes to the Sublime Porte for 25 years. What were the results of those official notes? At the bottom of each can be read one the following statements: "No reply received", "No result", or "A decree has been sent by the Sublime Porte, but its result is not known". We cannot find a single note that has achieved its aim or positive result. This means that in 25 years, the Sublime Porte has not satisfied the Patriarchate on a single matter. That is a very sad thing to see, as it proves how little the Sultan's government defends justice and rights and how little it cares for the non-Muslim people's peace and welfare.

Indeed, several things have occurred that, having invited the Sublime Porte's attention, have been worthy of the most important

---

40. By "Turkified" Raffi means 'turned Muslim' and assimilated into the dominant community.

decrees. But the issue of Shah Hussein is enough to show what value such decrees have for stopping oppressors in the provinces. The reader has already seen that the five high-ranking ministers and viziers (like Ali Pasha, Midhat, Hussein Avni and so on) have not been able, with their decrees, to have a robber chief like Shah Hussein stopped from carrying out oppression. No other outcome was possible, as anarchy plays a great role in Turkish local government, with government officials becoming more and more arbitrary and rebellious as their distance from Constantinople grows.

Maybe the Sultan's cabinet often wishes to provide his non-Muslim subjects with peace, security of life, property and honour, and perhaps they want to work to stop the injustice and punish the oppressors. But of what use are good intentions, if they are not implemented and, thanks to the arbitrariness of the provincial and county officials, remain unimplimented? The Sultan's most important firmans have as much significance in terms of the welfare of the oppressed people as a talisman, written by a priest, has for the health of a child—a talisman that is carefully kept by his devout mother and placed under his pillow so that he does not die.

The untidy and ridiculous state of such works in Turkey does not surprise us in the least, as it is typical and born out of the natural order of things. However diligent the Porte, however it tries, and no matter how often it scatters firmans over the people in an attempt to enforce rights and justice, it is all useless. This is because we are convinced that miracles can only happen from above, whereas the reform of a country begins at its roots. A harvest cannot be reaped from sown seed if the soil has not been prepared. Likewise, thousands of firmans always remain "dead letters" because the educational level of the masses does not correspond to the highest ideal.

Let us set aside philosophy for now.

It is impossible for all the officials in the provinces and counties to be unjust. It may be seen in the Reports that there are people who attempt to implement the decrees and try to stop the oppression, but their efforts are unsuccessful. This is because they often provoke the rage of fanatical Muslims and, as a result, they cannot retain their positions. The chief oppressors everywhere are the country's famous and influential people, who have the power over a pasha or provincial governor. The Muslim people's interests are linked to the main oppressors. In these kinds of circumstances, what can a powerless official from a weak and powerless country do? He is forced to "go with the flow", because to defend an oppressed Armenian against oppressive Muslims is the same as depriving the latter of his ill-gotten gains, which are even allowed by his religion and have taken root historically in his nature.

The ideal of Islam is close to that of oppression, which has been transferred to the masses via religion. Any religion will have the same influence, if its laws and doctrines do not have a general humanitarian application: in other words, if it makes a distinction between its believers and others. Some things that are forbidden for use against a Muslim are quite often permitted for use against a person of another religion. We could present hundreds of pieces of evidence, but one will suffice: according to sharia law, verbal testimony has the same strength and power as a written statement, but the testimonies of non-Muslims concerning Muslims are not acceptable. For this reason, every kind of crime can be hidden by this difference. A Muslim kills an Armenian; an Armenian girl is raped; something belonging to somebody has been stolen—all this happens in an Armenian area so, naturally, the witnesses will be Armenian. But as their testimony is not accepted, the crimes go unpunished. The testimony of a non-Muslim is only acceptable when it is given in favour of another Muslim. Consequently, Islam is the main stumbling block in bringing justice and civilian equality to Turkey. From this, it is understandable why reforms concerning Christians—which are often proposed with all sincerity to the central government—are never carried out.

If we accept the Patriarchate's Reports as the statistical record of the crimes carried out against Armenians in Asiatic Turkey, then the figures therein lead us to some very sad conclusions. Let us discuss them, one by one.

The religious conversions that took place in the 25-year period (only two people) hold the smallest place in the Patriarchate's records. Why? Some may think that only a few conversions take place and they do not involve the Patriarchate. Nonsense! They do take place and, if the Patriarchate has only two problems concerning them, it is for specific reasons.

Religious conversions in Asiatic Turkey do not take place because of belief, as Islam does not offer any advantage to the Christian Armenian to make him want to change his religion. It is sufficient to note the unfortunate story of Martha: religious conversions happen mainly to girls and women, and for the following reasons. In Asiatic Turkey, the number of villages inhabited only by Armenians is very small; many are mixed with Kurds and Turks. If there are completely Armenian villages, then Muslim ones are found nearby, while in towns the population is always mixed. For this reason, Armenian and Muslim relations are never in isolation. Different things happen as a result of such closeness. There's a saying among Muslims: "It is a good thing, but unfortunately it belongs to a non-believer". The Muslim always has his eye on all Armenian possessions—whatever is beautiful or precious. Beautiful Armenian women and girls could not fail to be attractive to them.

The Turk, and especially the Kurd, has a great appetite for things,—even more so, if they have been stolen. To steal a girl and make her his wife is not only considered a triumph for a Kurd, but also an act of bravery. The people who suffer through this bravery are Armenian women. A second, more powerful motive gives them a reason to kidnap them: religious fanaticism, because stealing Christian women and girls and turning them into Muslims has religious benefits.

Once the girl has been kidnapped from her father's home, there is no hope of her returning. Islam has dreadful laws for individuals who become Muslim (even if it is by force) and then revert to their old religion. Any Muslim meeting such a person has the right to kill them. Dread closes their way back to their previous lives.

Another form of fanaticism—this time practised by Armenians, which is no less fervent than that of Muslims—is chiefly responsible for the loss of those poor women. A girl or woman who has been kidnapped by a Muslim is considered a befouled person. They lose respect and personal honour in their community, and it is difficult to find an Armenian who would be willing to marry them. The poor women know this, and if they have the courage to escape the hands of their kidnappers, they never return to their relatives; they choose instead to hide their dishonour, commit suicide or, from despair, unwillingly bow before tyranny. Thus, the religious conversion of women is linked to kidnapping and rape.

Given these realities, it is obvious why religious conversions hold so little space in the Patriarchate's records. It is because the Patriarchate cannot protest, as there is no complaint from the people involved; they often remain silent about such events for the two reasons given above. If the story of poor Martha does not threaten the massacre of all the Armenians of Baiburt, it is hardly worthy of the attention of the Patriarchate or the governor of Erzerum.

These remarks are about women, but religious conversions among men take place for altogether different reasons. For example, often an Armenian will have a quarrel or trial with his relatives or community or wish to take vengeance on his enemy. To gain the backing of Muslims, he changes his religion, because Islam provides greater rights and easier ways to satisfy his evil passions. Another point is that if someone has committed a crime, by changing his religion, he can escape punishment. If he is lazy or poor, he can obtain his daily sustenance through religious conversion. The majority of men who change their religion are evil and immoral and, in Muslim circles, they gain satisfaction from their fanaticism.

We do not recognise any other reasons for religious conversion, as we know Islam has no missionaries. It is based on the sword and is preserved through fanaticism.

It remains for a few words to be said about the religious conversion of youths. The same happens to them as happens to young girls, as in the world of Islam they both have the same significance.

Apart from religious conversions, the Patriarchate's records devote little space to murders (i.e., only six people). This too is a very sad thing to see, and it explains the very poor state of Turkish Armenians. It is very sad to do so, but we repeat and doing so will raise a question against us—"Is it desirable to massacre great numbers of Armenians in Turkey?"

Although we ascribe the events in our lives and things that happen in nature to pre-ordained governance, we are convinced that everything has its real reasons. We could not ascribe a small number of murders among Armenians to the mercy of the Muslims, or assume that they are dealing with Armenians in a more humanitarian way, while the one is actually massacring the other in greater numbers.

Let us explain our thoughts.

The number, nature and types of crime committed in a society demonstrate that society's material and moral state. The reasons and motives for the crimes committed are as different from those of others as one society's cultural level and economic state compared to those of another.

It has been generally noted that there are more murders committed in a society where employment, just remuneration and security of life have not spread throughout all classes, and wherever the powerful crush the weak and take whatever profit they can. The image of that bloody situation is seen in Asiatic Turkey. Here, not only do particular thieves and robbers steal foreign goods, and not only do the darabeys rob the people, but groups of bandits (such as Kurdish marauders) take the offensive from one end of the country to the other, steal what they want and spread poverty and destruction everywhere. The smallest act of self-defence by a person being robbed means the end of his life. This is how murders occur.

Killings happen here during the looting of houses and in the defence thereof; the more stubborn the defence, the more numerous the killings.

By examining the figures in the Patriarchate's records, we arrive at another conclusion. The figures relating to oppression are hundreds of times greater than those for murder. What's the reason?

We cannot find a reason other than that the Armenian in Turkey never shows any resistance and plays only a passive role, allowing the Kurd or Turk to take his wife or his daughter or young son, just as long as they leave him alone. He allows them to take his earnings, and steal the piece of land left to him by his forefathers, just to save his own life. Thanks to this low and poor behaviour, few killings occur: the Armenian sacrifices his family, his house, his honour and everything that is sacred to him, just to save his life. He just has not the courage to relinquish his life and preserve his rights.

There are greater numbers of murders among Muslims, because they do not behave like Armenians. They know how to reply to evil with evil.

Some people may perhaps ask what the poor Armenian should do when the Turks and Kurds have swords, but the Armenians none. With what can the Armenian resist his militarised[41] enemy? He must bow to tyranny and permit them to rob him, just so he can keep himself alive. All of these thoughts are those of naïve people, who look at obvious and unjust things and consider them laws laid down

---

41. The word used her is 'zinvorvadz'—made to be a soldier.

by divine providence. But we do not believe that God has given the Turk and Kurd swords to rob Armenians, or that God is punishing them because of the nation's sins. The reasons behind the Armenians' slavery and their present faint-heartedness are so complex that we must look through their entire history to explain it; such analysis, however, is beyond the scope of our article. All we'll say is that if an Armenian, with a few lira in his pocket, instead of spending it on stock so that he can again make a profit, spends some of it to buy a weapon to defend himself and his goods, no one would forbid it. If he does not do this and, like a Jew, is always after profit, who is guilty when he is robbed?

It is a different thing if the government keeps all weapons in its possession, and retains the right to use them for itself, thereby superintending all its subjects' peace and security. But as Turkey does not have the power to do so, it therefore falls upon its subjects to protect themselves in whatever way possible.

"Let someone else cut it into pieces and I'll eat it", the Armenian saying goes. It is a lazy nation's saying, and the whole of its life-doctrine is encapsulated therein. The Armenian still waits; he waits with the patience of a Jew. If Christians were to be given peace at the price of another's blood, then perhaps the Armenian could be given some, too. It is a nice dream, if it comes true.

The Armenian, throughout his entire life, has behaved thusly: "Let someone else cut it into pieces and I'll eat it". His slavery is a result of following that policy. He not only has behaved like this in his political life, but in science, the arts and personal skills as well; for this reason, he's not produced anything and he's given nothing to humanity except his "Let someone else cut it into pieces and I'll eat it". We do not use very severe language in criticising this conduct among Armenians; we say only that begging is a characteristic of the lazy, and that a beggar's hunger is not usually abated by the crumbs from a foreigner's table.

Let us return to what we were discussing previously.

We said that the small number of killings of Armenians, according to the Patriarchate's records, demonstrates theslackness and slave-like mentality of even Armenians in reporting such crimes. To clarify this point even more, we feel that we should speak at some length about oppression and land problems which, comparatively speaking, occupy much more space in the Patriarchate's records.

* * *

The oppression of Armenians happens mainly in the north-eastern part of Turkish Armenia and, according to the Patriarchate's records, is centred in the regions around Lake Van. These regions include the provinces of Erzerum, Dikranagerd (Diarbekir) and Vasbouragan, and their respective counties. These are the regions most densely populated by Armenians and at greatest distance from Constantinople.

The oppression practised upon Turkish Armenians can be divided into three types. First, there is that which is carried out by government officials; secondly, that perpetrated by the Kurdish derebegs (tyrants and rebels) and by influential Turks; and, lastly, that by the ordinary Muslim population.

The greatest portion of the oppression carried out by government officials relates to government taxes and the tax collectors' pitilessness. There have been so many different kinds of taxes and ways to pay them that it is impossible to give any accurate information about them. This is because in each province, the amount of tax to be collected and the way to pay it depends on a tax collector's moral qualities, more so than the tenets of the law. But the people's protests have been mainly about the unjust division of taxation, which has meant that the amount due from Muslims has actually fallen on the Armenians. The Armenian is a tractable and docile porter who, with the patience of an ox, carries his burden, no matter how impossible it is, whereas the Turk may rebel and shake off the load placed upon him by a tyrant.

Military taxation placed on Armenians is one of the obligations that carry no rights with it. The Armenian, as we have pointed out, pays a tax instead of providing soldiers, and so he does not enjoy the special privileges accorded to the soldier-providing Muslims. For the Armenian, the military tax is in reality a type of fine that hurts him to pay, as it takes advantage of his stupidly forgiving nature.

When the question of military service in Turkey was first raised, our journals argued about it for a long time. I can still remember those inane arguments. Most of them can be summarised in the saying, "Let the Armenian pay rather than be a soldier; he can always use money, but for the Armenian, his blood is precious."

How frightened that nation is of blood, not realising that salvation itself costs blood!

Our nation's history teaches us that when the Armenians had troop contingents in the armies of the Persians, Mongols, Arabs and other governing powers, they fought not a little to protect their homeland from the barbarities of those powers in whose service they worked. And so, with the Armenian in the Turkish army, if he cannot provide any other assistance to his homeland, at least he'd learn that apart from bowing under slavery, there is another tool of self-defence—the weapon.

We are convinced that if the Armenians had soldiers in the Turkish army, the oppression taking place in Asiatic Turkey would be largely suppressed. This statement needs no drawn-out explanation; those who know Turkey and the sources of oppression will also be convinced, along with us, that only an armed man can oppose an armed Kurd and protect his home, family honour and so forth. If not, then keeping a Kurd in line by way of imperial firmans is impossible.

Our remarks were about oppression by government officials. After the question of military taxes, it can be seen that the next largest item in the Patriarchate's records concerns the 10-percent tax, collected from the harvest of cultivated crops. Here the poverty of the agricultural labourer suffers from extreme mercilessness. The peasant is required to pay two kinds of tax on the land under cultivation: the first is land tax and the other, 10 percent of all cultivated crops. This happens only when the cultivated land belongs to the person cultivating it but, as can be seen from the Patriarchate's records, the majority of Armenians' land has been appropriated by force by Turkish and Kurdish derebegs. In this case, the Armenian has become the derebeg's or his new agha's serf. The Armenian then has to pay four kinds of taxes for the land he cultivates, as he has two aghas: the government and his new landlord. He pays the government the land and 10-percent crop taxes separately, and then he must pay his landlord a separate land tax and the 10-percent crop tax for the same land as well. If you can imagine that cultivator's state, then it is clear why he leaves his plough and his homeland and emigrates to foreign countries to seek his fortune.

The methods of paying these taxes have significantly increased the cultivators' misfortunes. The government officials would give the 10 percent tax with interest to their relations and secretly become partners with them. The person (*multezim*) receiving the tax is as merciless as a robber or kidnapper, especially when his activities coincide with his interests. The Patriarchate's records have more than enough examples of how the tax collectors steal; they not only take the 10-percent tax, but also the proscribed so-called *shahnalik* and *olchek-hakke* taxes. If the crop has no value, it is left to rot in the cultivator's fields; in this case, instead of the usual 10 percent, the tax collector demands the tax in coin. When the cultivator has not got the money to pay the tax, they sell his vital agricultural tools and animals. This is the main reason that agriculture does not progress in Asiatic Turkey and why famine often occurs in the country. What can the cultivator do when the government itself, both directly and indirectly, steals the fruits of the farmer's efforts—and if anything remains, it is forcibly passed to the landlord, who had taken the land by force in the first place?

The brevity of our article does not allow us to enter into other details; suffice it to say that, in the same country, these things do not happen to the Muslim living on the same soil.

Government officials' judicial prejudice between Muslims and non-Muslims denies Armenians not a little of their rights, and the injustices done to them always remain unpunished. In these circumstances, the Armenian has only one way of getting justice on his side: by soothing the heart of a bribe-loving individual with silver. This works only occasionally, for after filling the purse of the judge with silver, he often still loses his rights. The judge always leans towards the side that has power, but in Turkey strength and power are only in the Muslim's possession. He enjoys legitimate privileges denied to Christians: he can, for example, produce innumerable witnesses to justify himself in a court of law, but an Armenian's testimony is not acceptable. (Testimony plays a part in Muslim written law). It was not very long ago that we read in the Constantinople newspapers about an event that had happened in the Van region. A Muslim, without written proof and with false witnesses at his aid, made an Armenian guilty of being in debt to him; having had him put in prison, they extracted a payment from him. In this way, every Muslim can rob an Armenian as he pleases; he never lacks witnesses and the judge assists in his crime, as some of the silver paid will belong to him.

The Muslim reads, on every Armenian's forehead, the following words: "giavour" and "rayah". This saying contains the entire doctrine of his belief; for him, the Armenian is nothing more than prey given to him by God, whom he then has the right to use for whatever purpose pleases him. The Muslim is not wrong in his idea; the Armenian, with his passivity, proves the Muslim correct.

Enough about government officials; let us turn to the oppression practised by individual tyrants (*derebegs*) and by the ordinary Muslim population.

There are more detailed accounts about this in the Patriarchate's records, with the majority of the protest notes to the Sublime Porte being about the oppression carried out in the provinces. The reader has already gained by this point a considerable idea of the kinds of oppression perpetrated, so we will not discuss them at length here; we wish only to show the sources from which the oppressions spring.

After the Armenians, the Kurds form the greatest minority in Turkish Armenia. They still live in a primitive fashion—a nation with no industry or farming—but consider robbery as a just reward and killing as bravery. The majority of Kurds are nomadic and, with their animals, they wander the Armenian highlands. A very small minority live semi-settled lives.

The feeble forces of the Turkish government were useless in conquering the wild Kurds, and the Tanzimat,[42] with all its humanitarian sentiments, was not able to tame these barbarians' mercilessness towards Christians. The Kurdish ashirets have always been unrestrained and continue their robberies to this day.[43] The government added to the Kurds the Circassians—those ferocious sons of the Caucasus who, in their way of living, are not so different from the Kurds themselves.

Under the oppression of the Kurds, rape, minor thefts and robberies have become so common that it would seem the people have become inured to them and do not consider them anything

---

42. Tanzimat was the era of Ottoman reforms beginning in 1839. These reforms covered a range of military, administrative and social issues to modernise the Ottoman Empire. These included measures to guarantee the equality of all Ottoman subjects. However, the failure of ensure equality between the Christian and Muslim communities of the Empire formed the social background to Raffi's commentaries in *Tajkahayk*.

special. For this reason, hardly anyone protests; they say, to comfort themselves, "Oh well, he's a Kurd, that's what he does". The wretch has no redress and is forced to remain silent. If he does protest, the Kurd, who today stole his sheep or ox, will return tomorrow and cut off his head.

The Kurd is not lazy in his profession; indeed, he is not satisfied with small thefts. Very often, organised groups comprised of hundreds of horsemen take the offensive against all the villages in a particular area, steal all the flocks of sheep and other animals and deprive the peasants of all their possessions. In those sorts of circumstances, the peasants usually say, "the knife has reached the bone",[44] and the people are forced to register a protest. But to whom? Who listens to their voices? The voice of the poor person is always smothered in his own breast.

It may be seen from the Patriarchate's records that the protests generally concern places that are near towns and cities, like Van, Moush, Paghesh, Dikranagerd, Erzerum and so on. This is not because more acts of oppression occur near cities; on the contrary, the closer to the city, the less oppression there is. There are, however, Armenian leaders and provincial pashas in cities, and the people can send their protests either directly or via their leaders to Constantinople. But in far flung corners—in other words, in places distant from the central towns and cities—even greater and more merciless oppression takes place, of which nothing is heard. This is because in those places, the poor people do not even know that there's a Patriarchate in Constantinople, that there's a Constitution, and that they can appeal there.

---

43. In Asiatic Turkey, and mostly in the Armenian regions, there are to be found, even today, places like, for example, Poulanik, where the Kurds retain a totally independent and rebellious state. In that area there are Armenians who live mixed with people of the Kurdish Chargha tribe and who cannot easily be distinguished from them. There the Armenians carry out robberies with the Kurds, taking the offensive in various directions and don't even spare their co-religionists. The resident Kurds on the Turkish-Persian border are almost totally in a state of uncontrolled rebellion and move across the border from whichever side creates problems for them. (Author's note)

44. The English equivalent would be 'Enough is enough'.

The Patriarchate in Constantinople, with its weak Constitutional administration, has not been able to be effective in all Armenian-populated areas of Asiatic Turkey even today. It is for this reason that mutual communication links have not developed between the people and the national administrative centre. I have personally had the opportunity to hear a poor Armenian's complaint about his situation. If you were to ask him why he has not protested, the usual reply is, "Whom shall I protest to?" The wretch does not even know that there are courts for the guilty; he only knows of one court, and that is heaven.

What need is there of protests when the people have had experience and know that their situation will only worsen if they complain? Protests being given no satisfaction either by the Patriarchate or the Sublime Porte, the only outcome is that the tyrant's vengefulness is provoked yet further, and—if he had any fear of prosecution before—his mind is now at ease, and he can torture his victims with even greater confidence. Under such conditions, there remains but one way out for the Armenian: to bow before his enemy's cruelty and completely surrender to his will.

Such cases can be found in the Patriarchate's records. All the Armenian villages and even the monasteries and churches become vassals of the Kurdish derebegs, Turkish tyrants and influential muftis and sheikhs. This is involuntary servitude, which the people pay in desperation to their oppressors, so that they will leave them in peace. In this way, the weight of two sorts of slavery are laid upon the people: that of the Turkish government, and that of the Kurdish or Turkish derebegs or independent tyrants. Not only a whole mass of people but also specific individuals who enter this or that influential Turk's or Kurd's protection so that others will not harm them are subject to this condition (especially if they are even somewhat wealthy). But this protection is very expensive; the persons or groups so protected, along with their houses and honour, become their agha's captive. That is a form of voluntary slavery in which the powerless subjects himself to the powerful and becomes a passive object of his will. That is the start of serfdom (*djordoutiun*), sad examples of which can be found in the Patriarchate's records. In the Mogk region, the Kurds of the town of Tinis buy and sell Armenians among themselves as serfs.

* * *

The Turkish central government, seeing that the barbarities perpetrated by the Kurds and other wild tribes arise from the nature of their nomadic life, has recently begun efforts to persuade them to leave their lives of wandering, leave shepherding, have settled homes and become farmers. It hopes in this way to subdue the Kurds and other wild tribes. The idea was not a bad one, but it was incorrectly implemented: instead of collecting the Kurds from the Armenian highlands and settling them in an area of Turkey that was unpopulated (such as the deserts of Mesopotamia or Assyria), the government allowed them to occupy areas in Armenia itself as settlement areas. How could this be?

The land was in the hands of the Armenians, left to them by their fathers and ancestors as inheritance. It was difficult for the Kurd to buy land from Armenians with money, as he was used to taking whatever he wanted from them by force. So he did the same again. It is from this land and property problem that a new form of oppression started.

In the records contained in the Patriarchate's first Report—in other words, until 1872—there were almost no land or property matters cited. This means that, until that year, the Armenians were the owners of their land and other property. This was the time during which the Kurds were still living nomadically and had not yet become concerned with land. But when, by government order, they gradually began to establish settled lives, the question of land was bound to arise.

This matter, as we have said, appeared after 1872 and is reflected in the records found in the second Report by the Patriarchate. Until then, the Kurds and other wild tribes were only concerned with stealing the Armenians' movable property, but after that date they began to also appropriate Armenian fixed assets. In various provinces, they forcibly took from the Armenians over 363 complete villages and the land belonging to them. The names of the provinces, villages and those of the usurpers are written down individually in the Report. In many cases, the villagers were dispossessed and thrown out of the villages by the Kurds, who took their land and made it their own. In some villages, however, some of the Armenians were permitted to remain, with only their land being taken and the Kurds becoming the landowners. Forcing the Armenians to accept this fait accompli, they then forced the Armenians to cultivate their ancestral lands on their behalf, taking taxes and 10-percent, and even taking as much as half the crop yield. Apart from the 363 villages and small towns, the Kurds also took over many areas of land belonging to a great number of Armenian villages in the counties of Seghert (Siirt), Charsanjak and Charshamba, whose names are not recorded.

The Kurds were not satisfied with just taking individuals' lands. They started to take over lands belonging to monasteries, with large areas belonging to 21 monasteries forcibly commandeered. Additionally, they demolished many monasteries, completely destroying their legacy.

It must be noted that the information contained in the records is mixed, concerning not only the ordinary Kurdish people, but also their begs, spiritual sheikhs and muftis, as well as Turkish aghas. Apart from this, there is information about various officials—officials who, as well as being tyrannical, have protection afforded them by the government.

Instead of stopping the aforementioned pillage and listening to the Armenians' protests, the central government looks on all these injustices with complete indifference. It even seems content with things being this way. It considers the Armenian its docile subject, and even if the Armenian has no land, he can be expected to look after himself—but the rebellious Kurd must, in some way, be tied to the land to stop him from moving about.

This idea is not without proof, as we see that the majority of Armenian-owned land is purloined by the government, which in turn is given to Muslims.[45] So that its injustice takes a legal form, the government created the fraudulent Tapou Law. On the basis of this law, every piece of land that has remained uncultivated for a number of years is considered mahloul or without an owner and therefore belonging to the state. This sort of land is taken by the government itself, and can then be registered to Muslims; for a very small fee, the

---

45. Government appropriated land is different to that belonging to villages, which we have mentioned. The tapou law is so complicated that a whole series of articles must be written to explain the spirit of this cunning land law, under which the land belongs to an individual only in name, being actually owned by the state. (Author's note)

Muslim can have an imperial certificate of ownership issued in his name. This is the reason Armenians are likely to lose the majority of their lands.

The reader may remember that we said that due to the 10-percent tax and extortion practised by the tax collectors, Armenians often left their land untended and emigrated to Constantinople or another city to work as porters or to do other heavy work to earn their daily bread. The land therefore remained without an owner, although the emigrant's family remained in their home near the land itself. In the eyes of the government, however, such land was considered without ownership, as there was no one to tend it. Bearing in mind the many emigrants (or refugees) in Asiatic Turkey—with at least 45,000 being found in Constantinople alone—it is understandable how much Armenian-owned land was left without owners and uncultivated. Considering these lands *mahloul*, the government sells it to the Muslims, and when the poor exiled Armenian returns, he finds himself deprived of his only inheritance and last hope.

The Turkish government does not even spare the land owned by monasteries or churches. The church and the monastery are considered, under this particular law, to be an abstract entity and cannot therefore be a landowner. Under this law, gifts of land bequeathed over the centuries by devout Armenians to secure the existence of the monasteries, fall into the hands of Muslims. To understand the enormous loss of national patrimony suffered by the Armenian nation, it is necessary to understand the great number of monasteries and the vast areas of land that belong to them in Asiatic Turkey.

Bearing thousands of misfortunes and all kinds of wretchedness with patience, the Armenian in Armenia had only one comfort: he was the master of the land. It had been irrigated with the sweat of his forefathers. But he was deprived of that comfort, too. On the one hand, the Kurd forcibly took his land, while on the other the government, stealing it, gives it to the Muslims. So what's left?

"The future of Armenians is in Turkey," say the short-sighted. We do not understand what future there can be in a country where there is no security of life or property. "It'll get better soon," the short-sighted imagine.

Those who do not admit to the devouring and destructive nature of the Muslim, deny both history and truth.

It is not possible to predict a rosy future for any nation if the economic basis of its existence is not stable, or if it is being materially and morally destroyed little by little and swallowed up by a more powerful element. The Armenian in Asiatic Turkey does not have a secure situation; the greatest proof of this is that he cannot support himself in his own homeland and whatever he makes is stolen from him, leaving him always poor and hungry and forced into exile to feed himself. The Armenian in Turkey lives in an uncertain situation. A plant like this cannot establish roots and soon withers.

There are, in Asiatic Turkey, two classes: the merchant and the cultivators. The latter, with both its great significance and sheer number, forms what we call "the masses". The merchant, on the other hand, is not comfortable in his establishment, and is always chasing after profit; he finds himself wherever it dictates. The merchant does not have a homeland; his country is where money is. The merchant has no regard for the welfare of the community: he is selfish. There remains the class of cultivators, which constitutes the bulk of the masses; they find no rest or livelihood in their homeland, so they too spend their lives in exile. Their strong hands, which should have cultivated the soil of their homeland, are used for low and servile work. The cultivator, the just husbandman, the one who provides the people's living, becomes a hamal, a porter, a beast of burden.

Thus the majority of the population in Asiatic Turkey lives in exile. Only one class remains immovable: that of the monks in the monasteries. But when the monasteries became subject to the same conditions as the people—when they too were shorn of their lands, their main source of wealth—the monastic orders also began to disperse and Armenian holy places became deserted.

The most important matter concerning the oppression of Turkish Armenians is about land or property. Its significance is so great that we believe the only way to stop emigration and have Armenians live safely in Turkey on their ancestral land is peaceful agriculture. But we regret to see that this matter holds a very insignificant place in the Patriarchate's Report. In the Patriarchate's 17-year stewardship under the Constitution, very little attention has been given to it and the land question has been practically ignored, although it is the matter of life or death for the Armenian. These words are not slanderous as we have, right in front of us, the Patriarchate's records.

The whole Report, as we recall, contains the record of 25 years of activity by the Patriarchate. In all of those 25 years, there was only one protest note issued by the Patriarchate about land extortion, and it was presented to the Sublime Porte on January 3, 1875. It too did not bring about any satisfaction, and the Patriarchate stayed silent on the subject thereafter.[46] On the contrary, we see that Giragos' daughter has been raped or kidnapped by Muslims; that Mardiros' sheep were stolen; or that the Turks have hung a cross from some church around the neck of a dog they are parading through the streets; these scandals have become the subjects of years of negotiation between the Sublime Porte and the Patriarchate. We are not saying that silence should be maintained about these matters, but that they should not have been given as much importance as they have. These things are odd incidents; they may happen today but not tomorrow. But when the Muslims appropriate all the Armenian villages in a province—that is a crucial and vital matter, because it leads to a whole mass of people dying materially and morally, and subsequent generations are deprived of food and therefore their lives. But the Patriarchate's attention is not held by this issue.

Having made these observations, we arrive at the sad conclusion that the Armenian Patriarchate of Constantinople and what is called the National Constitution have spent too much time preoccupied with empty matters and have shown very little understanding of the real needs of the nation and people. For the entire duration of the Constitution, the Patriarchate chewed and muttered over the affair concerning Boghos Vartabed and the issues concerning the Catholicoses of Sis and Aghtamar,[47] thus spending almost all its time engaged in pointless disputes; but one question never crossed its mind: why 45,000 hamals (porters) from Van, Moush and other

---

46. In the Patriarchate's last presentation to the Grand Vizier on behalf of the Armenians in Turkey on matters of concern, the overall subject of land was once more among them. However, only specific matters concerning the appropriation of church and monastery lands were cited. We are surprised that, if a specific individual holding office like Shah-Hussein and his exile from his homeland could turn into a public question, how much more should the problem of the appropriation of land capture the attention of the Patriarchate. (Author's note)

provinces had left their homeland and were languishing in Constantinople.

Although we know about the light-mindedness of the people of Constantinople, and although we know they are living in a dreamland and have no particular standpoint, we did not have such an unfavourable opinion of the Patriarchate and its constitutional administration. Their Reports, however, have exposed their irrelevance. If the current situation in Turkey did not provide the opportunity, we probably would never have seen the Reports. Maybe the Patriarchate would have kept its disgrace hidden in perpetuity, always deluding itself and presenting itself to the nation as doing great things.

It has not been long since that great deception—the notable circular from the Patriarchate—was published, in which the representative of about 4,000,000 people stated that he was content with the "benevolent government". The head of these people expressed his contentment, despite 25 years of continual protest against the injustices that never received redress. It is an incredible delusion.

The reader has already seen the gist of the protest notes presented to the Sublime Porte concerning oppression in the provinces; almost none achieved their aim, as some have remained without reply and others without result—or, if the Sublime Porte did issue a decree, provincial officials left it without any action being taken. So, in essence, all protests remained without result. It is from this that it may be understood what little significance the Armenian Patriarchate had for the Sublime Porte, and to what extent the Porte cares about the security of non-Muslim nations.

With things being like this, we have no right to expect miracles to be performed by the Patriarchate. But one thing amazes us: what is

---

47. The Catholicosate of Sis (in Cilicia) was co-equal with that of Etchmiadzin, although due to the political situation of the time it was eclipsed by both Etchmiadzin and, more importantly, by the Patriarchate in Constantinople. It exists today as the Catholicosate of the Great House of Cilicia in Antelias, Lebanon. The Catholicosate of Aghtamar (based on the island of that name in Lake Van) was of much lesser significance and was abolished in 1916.

the Constantinople Armenian National Constitution boasting about, with its 17-years of applause and rousing cheers?

Now we understand.

The Armenian National Constitution is nothing more than a toy, given to the child by a crafty nanny to keep him quiet and occupied, and to stop him from being naughty. The childish effendis are very pleased with this toy and celebrate their poor dreams every year near the Bosphorus.

The Turkish government understands the nature of the nations subject to it. It knows how to deceive each of them. It has now prepared an enormous toy to give to its subjects—a constitutional General Assembly. Let us express our opinion of this with a popular saying: "The snake sheds its skin, but its nature (khasiat) remains the same."

* * *

I had almost completed my article when I received a letter concerning the fire in Van. The writer was a person well known to me from that city, who had witnessed the event. Although the newspapers in Constantinople and Tbilisi carried articles about the fire, details were lacking. I feel, therefore, that it is necessary to include the contents of that letter as an addendum to my article.

The majority of the Armenian population of Van lives in the suburb called Aikesdan, at some distance from the fortress—in other words, at some distance from the city. The people of Aikesdan, both merchants and artisans, have shops in the fortress, coming to them in the very early morning, working there during the day and returning home at sunset. The shops are guarded by hashases (civilians hired for the purpose).

A few weeks before the fire, one of the Kurdish begs told Armenians he knew, in a friendly fashion, that they would be in great danger from the Muslims in the near future.

Even without this warning, the Armenians expected that the Turks would massacre them at any time, as the criminal Abd-ul-Fettah Beg, returning from Dikranagerd (Diarbekir), had long ago invited the Muslims to massacre all the Armenians.

The Armenian thinks about his wealth before his life, as the former is more precious to him. Hearing of this threat, the Armenians took no action to prevent the calamity from happening, but instead worked to save their possessions. The Armenians of Aikesdan took all their precious things to the city and put them in their shops, thinking that they'd be safer there than they were in the fortress, where there were soldiers, police and so forth. In this way, the Armenians' wealth was centralised in the market area.

During the night the hashases noticed that smoke was seeping out of this or that locked shop and understood that there was a fire. They hurried to let the shop owners know, but the police forbade it. At the same time, the sound of a bugle was heard from the roof of the barracks. The market area was immediately surrounded by troops. One contingent closed the entries to the streets and refused entry to Armenians, while another began to break down the shop doors— not only of those from which smoke was escaping, but also of those distant from the fire. The soldiers themselves set fire to the latter and, within a few hours, the entire market area was consumed in flames.

What happened to the things stored there?

Soldiers and police looted most of it. Before the fire took hold properly, a motley crowd was seen—Turks, Kurds and other Muslims—who, it appeared, knew beforehand that this was going to happen. Assembling from the nearby villages, they had hidden during the day in Turkish houses and took anything left after the soldiers and police had finished their looting.

A career of looting was open to the Muslims; only the Armenians were not allowed to approach.

The letter writer added that one of the wealthy Armenian merchants from the city offered the military officer in charge up to 500 lira just to rescue his books and other papers from his shop, but he was refused. The Armenians of Aikesdan understood nothing of the fire, as they were some distance away, while those of the city were not allowed near the shops.

And so, whatever was valuable was looted, but that which was considered useless was left in the fire. So that the fire would grow, flammable things were thrown onto it—gunpowder, oil and so on. Some of the loot was hidden in Turkish houses and some was taken to the nearby villages; there were several boats moored in port in the village of Avants for that purpose. Two thousand shops were looted altogether, of which 1,300 were not destroyed (only their doors were smashed in), while the other 700 were burned down. The shops among these belonging to the Turks had, in the letter writer's opinion, probably been emptied in advance of the fire.

In the opinion of the letter writer, this was not a chance happening, but a premeditated and previously arranged plot—the secret of which was kept by the local military command and local government officials. Sensing it, the village or town Muslims had assembled on the appropriate night to partake in the looting. The Turkish beg had made warnings for some time before the event, with no aim other than to scare the Armenians into bringing their housebound wealth to the market area. Although the Armenian people had suspicions of the Muslim mob, it had always regarded the government and its military strength as its protectors. For this reason, the market area was considered a safe place, as it was protected by police and *hashases*, and was located close to the barracks within the fortress.

Although the letter writer's supposition remains thus far uncorroborated, a number of facts lend credence to the idea that the fire was contrived to cover up responsibility for the looting. A few days before the fire, the soldiers had purchased twisted paper tapers and other flammable items. During the evening of the night of the fire, many of the soldiers, approaching this or that shop, pretended to want to buy something (just at the time the shopkeepers were locking up) and surreptitiously left burning items in them. The writer quotes a known proof of his statement that, when one shopkeeper was about to lock his premises, two soldiers approached and one asked about a particular item. On receiving it, the soldier ran off, with the shopkeeper in pursuit. He managed to retrieve it. Meanwhile, the other soldier, who had stayed near the shop, threw a wrapped item into the shop and went away. The merchant, returning to his shop, found among the cotton goods, a piece of canvas containing red-hot coals that had already started to burn the canvas they were wrapped in.

The other, which raised more suspicions, was that the leaders of the looting, who were soldiers, were changed for new arrivals on the morning of the fire and left the city. This change was for no other reason than to obscure the trail of the robbers and to hide the criminals in the present military upsets in Turkey.

In the opinion of the letter writer, this act was not without an object. Apparently the Turkish government, in its current critical state, harboured suspicions about the Armenians living in Van.

Maybe they would go over to the Russians if a war were to occur, and it was for that reason that they thought of materially weakening them. In our opinion, that speculation is incorrect, as the Turkish government knows the Armenians very well. It knows how the Armenians fit in with its tyranny. It knows what sort of heart the Armenians have. We look on this as a cunningly planned looting incident and nothing more.

The writer has difficulty calculating the losses suffered, but thinks that it must be large, as trade in Van is in the hands of the Armenians, and Van is the centre of trade for the surrounding areas.

In the fire of Van, we see the same things as with the other examples of oppression in the provinces, where killings are at a minimum. In this case, too, there were no killings; it appears that the Armenians, in their fatefully poor-spirited manner, looked on to see how they were robbed. But the Armenians are more numerous in Van than the Muslims. In the battle for life, the Armenian has his own unique weapons to redress his losses. The Armenians of Van telegraphed their comrades in Constantinople: "They robbed us here; do not pay for any merchandise you've obtained from anyone."

It is inappropriate at present to pass more judgements on the fire in Van, as not everything has yet been clarified. It has already been announced by the Constantinople press that the Sublime Porte has already appointed a committee to inquire into this incident. We'll wait until the committee has finished its work, although we are convinced that the whole truth will never be revealed.

January 10, 1877

WHAT ARE THE REFORMS NEEDED IN TURKISH ARMENIA?[48]

If the present is a continuation of the past, and if we must take advantage of the past to correct the present, we would not be wrong to say that the Reports published by the Patriarchate in Constantinople—which contain the records of a quarter of a century's work in Turkish Armenia—are enough to give us an idea of the reforms the Armenian Patriarch must demand, so that Armenians may thereafter live in security and be free of the injustices perpetrated on them to this day.

In examining the Reports published by the Patriarchate, we can see that it mainly covers four key points: (a) lack of security regarding livelihood and property; (b) lack of security regarding human life; (c) lack of justice in the courts and the trampling of rights; and (d) lack of security safeguarding national peculiarities. To improve the lot of Armenians in Turkey, reforms can only be considered successful if they satisfy the above four points.

Let's talk about each point separately.

a. We do not regard insecurity of livelihood and property as the manner in which the Armenian is exploited, his labours are taken from him, and how he is always subject to various forms of violence and robbery. No! The lack of security of property, and therefore the difficulty in making a living, is mainly due to the fact that the Armenian has no land and for this reason has no stable basis for his life. Muslim law concerning land is part of the problem: "The whole

---

48. "Inch Norokutiuner", *Mshak*, 1878.

universe belongs to God, the Sultan is God's caliph or representative on earth, and the land belongs to him." It is from this idea that the ridiculous notion arises that, on whichever country's soil the Muslim ruler treads, such land belongs to him.

All the laws pertaining to land stem from this doctrine. The Sultan owns the land and the cultivator, or peasant class, is his tenant or tax gatherer. For the Armenian to have land, he must rent it from the government or, using the Turkish idiom, he must make it *tapou*. Otherwise, his rights over his rented land cease from the day he does not renew his land deed or does not carry out this or that duty. A land deed with such conditions has no more power than a written agreement.

Thus, there is nothing to tie the peasant class to the land and therefore to cultivating or working on it. Taking into consideration the unbearable conditions that weigh heavily on the cultivator in working a patch of land, it is quite understandable why he leaves his homeland in his thousands and emigrates to seek a livelihood in foreign lands. To tie the Armenian to his ancestral land, to stop emigration, the imperative—and only way to do so—is to give him the right to become a freeholder of land as his own property and gain the right to profit from it in every way. It is only in this way that the peasant may earn his living by his own efforts. He must not be a tenant; the land must be his certain inheritance that has passed down through the generations, which he can buy, sell or use as collateral: in other words, he must be able to use it as he would his own property. This must be one of the most important reforms demanded by the Armenian Patriarchate; if it wants Armenians to set down roots on the soil of Armenia, it must exercise authority over the Armenian nation and it must get nourishment from it, like a baby from its mother's breast. We regard the extortions carried out by the *multezims* (tax gatherers)—the weight of taxes under which the peasant class is being robbed—and the oppression carried out by various tyrants and derebegs as temporary irregularities from which not even the Muslims are exempt. They can only be rectified and brought within the law by general reforms in Turkey.

b. The insecurity of Armenian life due to constant harassment by the Kurds, Circassians and other wild tribes was the main basis of Article 16 of the Treaty of San Stefano, as well as that of Article 61 of the Treaty of Berlin. But it is impossible, no matter how hard the government of Turkey works, to protect the unarmed Armenians from the barbarities of the armed Muslims, as the whole of the military force that must be used for that purpose comprises those same barbarians. For this reason, the Armenians must be permitted to protect themselves, and that is only possible if the right is given for the Armenians to bear arms, like their neighbouring races, as well as allowing them to enter the Turkish armed forces. The Armenian must rely on himself for self-defence when the government cannot defend him. Those who are familiar with the organisation of Turkey will agree with us that it is impossible to live and preserve one's existence without weapons. Races that inhabit Turkey fight one another incessantly and compete with one another only with the sword. With what can the unarmed Armenian resist?

Armenian participation in the Turkish armed forces must be one of the greatest duties that the Armenians should perform, and not only as Turkish subjects and citizens; doing so would also free them from external enemies during wartime, and internal enemies during peacetime. In place of military service, Armenians pay a tax to the Turkish government; that same tax could be used to maintain a national militia.[49] We're asked: why specifically a militia? Why should Armenians not join the Turkish armed forces?

As far as we are aware, none of the specific nations—Kurds, Circassians, Arabs and so on—do Turkish military service, nor do they enter the ranks of the regular army. Instead, they form separate militias that, after wartime, return to their homes. Additionally, Armenians cannot enter the Turkish regular army as soldiers, as various religious differences prevent the two races from mixing or having close relations with one another. Turkish soldiers do not want non-Muslims in the ranks at all.

---

49. The author is referring to an Armenian militia.

If the demand is made for the Armenians to provide regular troops rather than a militia, then the Armenian soldiers should form separate regiments with their own Armenian officers and generals within the Turkish army. That is how it always was; after the passing of the Arshagouni kingdom,[50] during the whole of the Marzban era,[51] and in the times of Arab, Tatar and Greek[52] domination, Armenian troops always served as a separate corps in other powers' armies, with their own officers.[53] They even took *kahanas* (married priests) and a Christian altar with them.

All the means currently used by the government to protect Armenians from the various wild tribes are useless. The Armenian must be given the means to protect himself, which will only happen when he is given the right to bear arms. It is altogether different if the government disarms all its subjects and every individual finds security of life and protection under it. But the government of Turkey cannot and does not want to do anything like that. When, a few years ago, the subject of disarming the Kurds was mooted, one of Turkey's prominent state figures, Ali Pasha, said, "It is not necessary; the Kurds are an ever-ready army for us." Yes, a ready army that lives off unarmed citizens who are used by the government, as it did in the last war.[54]

It would be superfluous for us to give advice, as we know that the Constantinople Patriarchate is well aware of the importance of an Armenian militia in protecting the country against its internal

---

50. This indigenous Armenian kingdom is known to history as that of the Arsacids, and lasted from 52–428AD.
51. Marzban era: marzban is best translated as military governor. Altogether the era lasted from 428–885AD; first under the Persians (after the division of Armenia between the Byzantines and Persians by the Peace of Apamea (Acilesene) in 387AD) then under the Arabs (from 640–885AD).
52. i.e. Byzantine.
53. During the time of His Imperial Majesty the Persian Shah, when Armenian soldiers were called up, they were formed into separate regiments under their generals. Not even the Persians permitted the Armenians to mix with them. (Author's note)
54. The author must mean the Russo-Turkish war of 1877–1878.

enemies; the provision for one has been inserted in the provisions of the Treaty of Berlin. But the demand must be made once more for the tax that Armenians pay in lieu of military service to be used to maintain militias in their own regions, to protect the country against internal attacks in peacetime, and to assist the government during wartime. We cannot see any other form of protection against the barbarities of the Kurds, Circassians and other wild tribes.

c. With regard to non-Muslims, the lack of protection of rights and justice always reign in the courts, as the sharia law is used in court cases. If we think that a law cannot be permanent, that it must gradually change and be perfected as man's life changes and improves as his needs and demands receive new forms, we can boldly state that the centuries-old, worn-out sharia laws are not sufficient and do not correspond to the requirements of not only the non-Muslims, but even of those of the Muslims themselves, whose patriarchal way of life has changed beyond all measure, from the day the laws were published by the Prophet of Islam's lips and were transcribed into the Koran. Unchanging and permanent laws, which are given to peoples ruled by God, are no more or less than huge fetters that impede and fossilise nations into eternal immobility.

It is difficult to demand that Turkey changes sharia law, as it has close links with the Muslim religion. But it is possible to demand that it remains unused in the case of Armenians and non-Muslim peoples. There is no other way, as there are many principles in it that are against the ideal of equality and these principles treat all the nations that are not Muslim differently. If until today all the sultans' *khadi*s and *firman*s remain unfulfilled, it is because of the powerful resistance of sharia law and nothing else.

So by what means can we be free of sharia law?

Truth demands that we must confess that the government of Turkey considered very early on that, as far as possible, non-Muslims and Armenians in particular should be free from the constraints of sharia law. This fact is evident by the permission given to the Armenians by the Turkish government for their own constitutional administration. Apart from this, in the provinces, *medjlis*es (special mixed assemblies) of Muslims and non-Muslims were convened to examine local affairs, so that non-Muslims would have nothing to do with *ulemas*[55] and *ghazis*.[56] In any event the Armenian Constitution and the local *medjlises* could not satisfy the Armenians. Why not? Because the Armenian National Constitution had a more ecclesiastical nature and did not go beyond dealing with Armenian national activities such as schools, the Church and so forth. On the other hand, the provincial medjlises, in their disorganised state, did nothing to help.

In our opinion, to demand something new so that the Armenians could free themselves from the injustices of the Turkish government courts would raise new difficulties; maybe they would not allow it. It is necessary to demand that they complete and perfect those privileges that they had once granted to Armenians on an incomplete basis. We refer once more to the Armenian National Constitution and provincial medjlises.

If the Armenian National Constitution were to widen its narrow remit with the addition of new rights and be given new political rights—if coming out from behind the walls of Constantinople it were to spread throughout all the Armenian-populated provinces—an Armenian administration could be set up encompassing Church, political and criminal matters, giving satisfaction to all. The Armenians, being ready for such an administration, would arrange matters among themselves with their own hands. But after this were to happen, a question arises: how and where would matters between Armenians and Muslims be decided?

The answer is simple: in the provincial medjlises.

The aim of the provincial medjlises, as we stated above, was to decide on matters pertaining to various nationalities; to that end, Muslim and non-Muslim members are elected to it. But if until today the medjlises have not achieved their aim, the reason is that they have no definite statute. There is nothing in writing; examination of any matter is carried out verbally and decisions are reached by vote—not by a majority but by what position the voter has taken in the medjlis.

---

55. *Ulema*: Islamic Council.
56. *Ghazi*: Islamic conqueror.

In these circumstances, as is well known, whims play a great part and matters are decided for the benefit of those people who have powerful protectors in the medjlis; powerful protectors may be Muslim, as non-Muslims are only present for appearance's sake.

From this it may be seen that the Turkish government has laid the basis for those institutions that would improve the non-Muslims' state, but which are as yet disorganised and without rules. It granted the Armenians a National Constitution, but it is incomplete; it set up mixed assemblies (medjlises), but without statutes.

Assemblies comprised of Muslims and non-Muslims can achieve their aim only if they are based on the principles of European legislation, and when they have a new organisation. The demand for such a court was contained in the plan presented by the Armenian Delegation to the Congress of Berlin, but it was strictly Armenian. In our opinion, Turkey must not be frightened that some new thing is being demanded of it. It is only necessary to change the forms of existing things and those once granted. The Constantinople Patriarchate must follow this policy in its demands for reforms: widening the narrow Armenian National Constitution with new rights and spreading it throughout all Armenian-populated provinces will be enough to allow the Armenians to deal with things themselves. Reforming the provincial medjlises will facilitate their judicial relationships with other nationalities.

d. Insecurity of national peculiarities. Speaking of national peculiarities, the Turkish Armenians' situation presents a very poor picture. Until now we have false impressions. We thought that "The Armenian nation is of one religion, based on its Church; and the Church will remain firmer in Turkey, so our nationality will be able to survive there." "If our nation exists today, it is thanks to Islam": so says one of our prominent thinkers.

We'll leave the argument against that idea, because the Armenian nation is not a religious entity; we'll leave the refutation of such a judgement, as a nation cannot survive forever based only on religion and it is virtually impossible for the Church alone to preserve nationality. Let us accept that the Armenian can remain Armenian with his religion and Church—but where is the Armenian Church and religion under such threat, if not in Turkey?

As to how Islam is swallowing up Christian races, it is sufficient to see the many "Islamised" Armenian villages that are everywhere in Asia Minor. But there is another, more potent threat to the Armenian Church—the Christian missionaries, who are more skilful than the Muslims, who make converts by preaching, whereas the Turks do so by force. In no other country have catholicism and protestantism spread so much among Armenians as in Turkey. Their preachers have reached almost everywhere. So how can people think that our Church is safe in Turkey? Conversions will increase when the British, taking Asia Minor under its influence, allow their missionaries to travel among the Armenians.[57] The preachers who have appeared so far have been Americans, but the arrival of the British will add to their numbers. It will be easier for the latter to hunt for converts, as we know that the Armenians who convert and leave the Armenian Church do so to obtain protection from Muslim-led persecution, rather than from religious conviction, and the British are able to protect their co-religionists.

It would seem that crafty Turkish policies have understood very well the importance of religious conversion among its subject Christian nations. Seeing, for example, the Armenians as a religious community—and one which did not recognise any other basis for its nationality except the Church—the government has always tried to keep it busy with religious dissension and always tried to destroy its unity, permitting the dissemination of catholicism and protestantism. Sultans in the past had hit upon a better basis for nationality—language, thanks to which so many Turkish-speaking and Kurdish-speaking Armenians appeared who are, nonetheless, adherents of the Armenian Apostolic Church. During the times of the recent sultans

---

57. I had the opportunity of talking to an English priest in Tabriz before the Russo-Turkish war, who was returning from Turkish Armenia. He stated that in London there was the intention of sending a mission of preachers to Armenia. This man had been sent to explore the possibility… (Author's note)

the strength of the Christian nations began to slacken and their national unity to split through religious discord.

Turkish policy was not satisfied with new Churches being formed among Armenians, but it attempted to sow discord among them, too, as happened between the Armenian Protestants and Armenian Catholics. It is sufficient to recall the Hassounian and anti-Hassounian feud that lasted for several years. If the government helped the anti-Hassounians, it was not because it was in favour of its more liberal aims, but that they wanted to form a new split among the Armenian Catholics, somewhat reducing their strength.

We generally regard Turkish policy as being more naïve than it actually is, overlooking the way it has grafted Byzantine cunning onto Mongol duplicity. The Turks know how to sow trouble between their subject races and how to sever their unifying links. Anyone who has studied the Armenian newspapers published in Constantinople remembers how a split in the Monastery of the Two Jameses in Jerusalem became the subject of contention between the Armenian Apostolic and the Greek Patriarchates in Constantinople. Every year, on Resurrection Day, scuffles break out between Greek and Armenian monks there. Quite often these scuffles lead to bloodshed. But in all these years, the government did nothing to put an end to these disputes, although they really were about small things.

We think that the reader will now agree with us as to the danger hanging over the Armenian Church in Turkey; if it is to be the basis for the preservation of the Armenian nation, its life is in serious doubt. According to the Treaty of Berlin, "freedom of religion" will give European missionaries a new field of endeavour, and the Armenians, with the hope of obtaining British protection for themselves, will sacrifice their religion. Who can compete with them? Our indifferent clergy or our foppish students? No one, in our opinion. It now remains for Armenians in Turkey to leave the Church, to leave religious beliefs to the individual's conscience and hold out our hands to the Armenian Catholic, the Armenian Protestant and the Armenian Muslim and say: "We're brothers, we must share our present and future and not let the Church divide us. Let us unite our strength and work together."

In ending this chapter, we summarise our thoughts as follows. The Armenian Patriarch of Constantinople, who is occupied with reforms to be given to the Armenians, should in the first instance unite with the Armenian Catholic and Armenian Protestant representatives and, as a general national collective, must have regard for the following main demands: (a) the peasant cultivator should own his own land and be given the security to remain free from tyrants and robberies by extortionists; (b) the Armenians should have the right to bear arms like neighbouring nations[58] and, instead of paying tax in lieu of military service, should be able to use the same money to maintain a national militia to protect themselves and their property from the various wild tribes—the Kurds, Circassians and so on; (c) to perfect the Armenian National Constitution by adding new rights and privileges and for it to be spread throughout the Armenian- inhabited provinces; (d) to make such arrangements so that the nation and its national peculiarities are preserved, that Muslim fanaticism is curbed and that forced conversions, kidnappings and rapes are put to an end. In addition, that the underhand methods used by Turkey to limit the progress of monasteries and schools should be abolished, so that study and education may be furthered without constraint.

It is time to shake off the dust of prejudice. It is time to take schools in hand, so that a new link can be forged between us and those people of Armenian nationality who have become foreigners to us, such that a new font, in which the Armenian Catholic, Armenian Protestant and Armenian Muslim may be baptised with a new spirit and a new life, and be anointed with the name of nationality. It is only in this way may we all be united with our brothers, while separated by our respective Churches

---

58. The original says "races".

THE KURDISH UNION[59]

The Sublime Porte, during the last meetings of the Congress of Berlin, created the Albanian Union as a method of creating difficulties for the European powers in the face of their demands and to reject, in a way, the decisions concerning Greece and Montenegro. To stifle the Armenian Question in its cradle, the Sublime Porte attempted to create a Kurdish Union.

It was only a few months ago that the Constantinople Turkish press shamelessly began to trumpet the wonders of the civilisation of the Kurdish element of the Empire, trying to present them before the eyes of Europe - these wild animals living in the mountains of Armenia - as enlighteners not only of the east, but of the west, as well. This kind of childish trick on the part of the Turkish press is beneath all criticism, this press which at one time was demanding the complete destruction of the Kurds as a useless and dangerous element, so that the eastern borders could be freed from their continuous marauding.

Sultan Abdul Medjid appeared as a dangerous instrument to annihilate the Kurds and their fate would have been the same as the massacre of the Janissaries, if the Grand Vizier and diplomat of the time, Ali Pasha, had not been able to calm his anger. The sly vizier was able to persuade the occupant of the throne of the caliphs with the thought that, although the Kurds were robbers, they were ever-ready soldiers for Turkey and that the government must make allowances for their indiscipline, so that they had the means to live and, when required, be brave warriors.

---

59. "Krdagan Miutyun", *Mshak*, 1880.

Those allowances proved very expensive for the government. While laying waste to entire provinces on the border, leaving the people there in dire poverty and disrupting agriculture and trade, not only did the Kurds not pay any taxes, but at the same time prevented government coffers from receiving any income from those provinces those savages had looted.

Sultan Abdul Aziz's government came to the conclusion that to restrain the Kurds, it needed them disarmed and made into settled farmers, rather than permit them to continue their tented, wandering existence as herdsmen. Every effort made was unsuccessful and the Kurds always remained vagabond shepherds who, with their animals, wandered the breezy mountains of Armenia during the summer, while in winter they descended to the warm plains of the Tigris valley. As to their being disarmed, that too remained without result, without even taking into account that one of the pashas of Van devised a ridiculous tax that the Kurds had to pay if they wanted to stay armed.

It was during this time that the government began to put pressure on the Kurdish tribal chieftains. The exile of Batirkhan-beg and the slaying of most of his tribe must be considered as one of the greatest blows struck by the government against the Kurds at any time. After that, the Kurdish chieftains became, in the hands of government representatives, a source of profit. They were imprisoned, tortured and exiled; all this was done, not to pacify the country, but for the profit it brought to the pashas who, accepting bribes, released their prisoners. This method of maintaining law and order gave the Kurdish robbers the opportunity to continue their plundering with even greater zeal to assure themselves of the capital needed to buy their freedom should they be arrested again.

In Kurdish understanding, those unjust pressures and continuous persecution nurtured a fierce hatred of the Turkish government specifically and of the Turks generally. Their usual mode of life was disrupted and they were denied their sources of income—pillage— which, according to Kurdish tribal and traditional custom, was not an altogether immoral trade.

That hatred towards the Turks gave the Kurds the opportunity to get closer to the Armenians and to become more familiar with them.

The whole Kurdish people, split between many and mutually antipathetic tribes, made it impossible for them to unite to form a union to fight against government pressures. Being protected by the Armenian mountains, they took their revenge, as far as it went, in despoiling one part of the country and moving like a flood to another, while the local authorities, with their powerless efforts, were never able to put an end to their continuous invasions.

Among these tribes there were those who were, relatively speaking, milder in nature and who, as simple shepherds, lived a simple patriarchal life. The chieftains of these tribes often approached Armenian effendis and leading clergy for assistance and protection against the whims of Turkish governors. The Armenian effendis and leading clergy, who were more significant in the eyes of the government as the representatives of the most important and largest community, did not spare their protection—although that protection could not have been pleasing to the Armenian people, who generally and historically hated all the Kurdish tribes. That was the reason that a large party was formed against the prelate of Van, Boghos Vartabed, because he defended the Kurdish chieftains, maintained friendship with them and, when they were arrested, freed them from prison using his own means. For ten years, the Armenians of Van were divided into two parties, one of which worked to get the Kurd-loving prelate removed from his post, while the other worked to keep him. These arguments occupied the Constantinople Armenian press for a long time and created not a few concerns for the Patriarchate.

The protection of peace-loving Kurdish tribes by Armenian effendis and leaders occurred for no other reason than the fact that the merchants had trading links with those tribes, supplying them with the necessities of life; they received, in return, the fruits of their pastoral existence such as oil, wool and animals. It is easy to see that the government officials' robbing of the Kurds harmed the interests of the Armenian merchants—Armenian capitalists—because the Kurds always owed them money.

These relationships created close allegiances between several Kurdish tribes and the Armenians and took on a friendly character the more the Turks put pressure on them. But there were tribes that were against the Armenians; they were as much against the Armenians as they were against their own people. It happened not a little that one Kurdish tribe attacked another and robbed it, in this way the fighting, massacre and intransigence among them remained a legacy from one generation to another.

Armenians were also involved in those disputes. The Armenians of Aghpag, Shadakh, Bulanekh, the region of Mogk and Sassoun all had their Kurdish tribal allies, with whom they united to fight a common enemy. The "Yezedi" non- Muslim Kurdish tribe, always harassed by Muslim Kurds, maintained friendly relations with the Armenians. The Armenians had such trust in that tribe that they handed over their animals to their shepherds to be taken to pasture, and the servants and maids in Armenian houses and cultivators of Armenian fields were mostly Yezedis. They carried out several Armenian religious ceremonies, kept the feasts of St. Sarkis and St. George, presented sacrifices to famous Armenian pilgrimage sites and regarded St. Gregory the Illuminator and the prophet David as the foremost among the chosen of God. Almost all the Yezedis knew how to speak Armenian and only one of our doctors of theology (who received, from the Armenian clergy, the facetious soubriquet of "miracle-worker") thought to spread Armenian Apostolic Christian teaching and literacy using the Armenian alphabet among them.

Kurdish and Armenian relations were like this until the start of the last Russo-Turkish war.

During the war, the Turkish government gave it a purely religious nature; by using *sheikh*s, *mufti*s and *ghazi*s, it was able to fire the Kurds' fanaticism. All the Kurdish bandits who, in their thousands, went to fight against Der-Ghougasov's regiments,[60] fought under their religious leaders (such as Sheikh Djelaleddin[61] and Sheikh Ibatullah).

---

60. Der-Ghougasov was a Russian commander on the Caucasian front during the Russo-Turkish war of 1877-1878. He was of Armenian extraction.
61. See Raffi, *Jalaleddin*, translated by Donald Abcarian, London: Taderon Press, 2006.

Although the Kurdish bandits were not able to give any notable help and looted, destroyed and burned areas of Turkey that still had not been captured by the Russians, they gained the interest of British agents who were spread throughout the Turkish armies in Armenia.

The British found that there were two main races in Armenia: the Kurds, who hated the "giavours" and joined the Turkish army; and the Armenians, who were sympathetic to the "giavours" and did everything in their power to support the Russian victories. Kurdish antipathy and Armenian sympathy toward the Russians—these two opposing manifestations were enough to give the British a false idea around which to implement their plan for Armenia.

The British did not want to think that, if the Turkish Armenians had pro-Russian sympathies, there was a natural reason for such sympathies—that they saw that their fellow-Armenians in Russian Armenia were in a more favourable state, while they themselves were disintegrating and disappearing from one day to the next thanks to the barbarities of a lawless and perfidious government. If that government were to change for the better, there is no doubt that the Armenians would be reconciled to it.

The condition of the Armenians did not really interest the British. They were looking for something necessary to them—a powerful barrier to be built against the Russians, to seal the road to their future conquests in Armenia and to prevent their movement towards the valley of the Euphrates. In this way, they considered that they would secure their interests in India. That barrier, in the opinion of the British, could only be formed out of the Kurds, because they could not trust the Armenians or depend on them, especially as they found the Kurds more suitable to their aims, the Kurds being already armed, while the Armenians were not.

That was the reason why, during the war, when British consuls were appointed in various Armenian cities, the first concern of Beaconsfield's[62] government representative, Layard, was to have Armenia named Kurdistan and to found a Kurdish Union.

---

62. Benjamin Disraeli, Lord Beaconsfield, Prime Minister of Great Britain.

After the war, the British consuls began to evince special interest in the Kurdish element of the population, with the aim of forming the imaginary Union among them. They began to bring them forward and push the Armenians back. They began to cultivate friendships with tribal leaders and sheikhs and employ every means at their disposal to try to unite the forces of the mutually hostile tribes. Doing so was not difficult; it was impossible. It was not possible to make centuries of inherited intransigence among hundreds of Kurdish tribes suddenly disappear through a miracle of British diplomacy, especially as the wild Kurd could not grasp the niceties of statesmanship. The result of all those efforts was that the Kurds, seeing that they were an object of attention, became bolder; as a result, just when the Russian army was in San Stefano, they began to massacre the Armenians in the Khnous area. Meanwhile, Sheikh Ibatullah destroyed over 50 Armenian villages in the Aghpag region's Bashkale area, and was rewarded with a cordial visit by the British consul in Van.

After the fall of the Beaconsfield government, the imaginary barrier—that artificial edifice—fell of its own accord. The ideal of the Kurdish Union disappeared into thin air, but the name Kurdistan remained. The British were not able to recover their losses.[63]

When, during the final conference prior to signing the Treaty of Berlin, the questions of Greece and Montenegro were tabled, and when the European ambassadors presented their united text to the Sublime Porte concerning the reforms in Armenia, the Turkish government reluctantly remembered the Kurdish Union, which was born of the Beaconsfield ministry. We say "reluctantly", because the Union could not have been something pleasant to the Turkish government that had tried, for many years and by artificially sowing discord among the Kurdish tribes, to engineer splits among them so as to destroy their unity, weaken them and, by so doing, reduce the Kurds to a subject and vassal people.

---

63. The expression used here is "The British weren't able to lick up what they had spat."

However, bearing in mind the circumstances, politics demanded that an obstacle be presented to the Europeans.

At that time, as we recalled above, the Turkish press had begun, on the one hand, to fan the Kurds' dark fanaticism and on the other hand trumpet the value of their culture, literature, schools, trades and so on—all of which had substance only in the imagination of *Vakit* and *Hakikat*. The Turkish press began to criticise the "wild" Armenians who were "barbarously" practising extortion among the "poor" Kurds. In other words, it was protesting that the lambs were devouring the wolves.

The Sublime Porte had not yet provided an answer to the united text presented by the ambassadors about the Armenian reforms but, suddenly, Kurdish delegates appeared in Constantinople, apparently sent by Sheikh Ibatullah[64] (but in reality engineered in the capital); presenting themselves to Abedin Pasha, they demanded autonomy for the Kurds and Kurdistan (changed from "Armenia").

What does this trick mean?

The question is quite simple. The whole issue was about the autonomy of, and reforms in, Armenia (or in Turkish eyes, Kurdistan). If autonomy was to be given to the region, why not grant it in the name of the Kurds, who were the rulers of the area and the region's original inhabitants, and whose culture (sic) was superior to that of all other races, especially that of the Armenians?

---

64. Sheikh Ibatullah, that false representative of the Kurds in Turkey was, in reality, the chieftain or, in other words, the mullah or religious leader of a tribe that was subject to the Shah of Persia. He and his tribe wandered from place to place on Persian territory, sometimes in the regions of Ulni or the province of Tarr and occasionally of Marr. During the Russo-Turkish war he was the leader of one of the Kurdish groups of bandits that attacked Bayazid. He gained notoriety there, inviting the attention of the Turkish government upon himself. At the time that his apparent representatives were in Constantinople, he was in Persia and possibly didn't even know that negotiations were being carried on in his name with the Porte. We will see that he began his disorders in the province of Sovough-Boulagh in Persia. (Author's note)

The European ambassadors, of course, took no notice of these points put forward by Abedin Pasha, and so the Kurdish representatives achieved nothing.

After this, the author of the Albanian Union, Abedin Pasha, began to dream about a Kurdish Union, and so the Turkish press accordingly began to change its tune. It was not really possible to represent the Kurds as a cultured, educated, freedom-loving and moral people. It also was not possible to say that the Kurds were good, upright and pitiable, and that the "wild" Armenians were oppressing them. It was necessary to portray them as unmerciful animals, as barbarian fanatics who were ready at any time to massacre every Armenian if autonomy for them was even mentioned.

In all of this, there was the thought that they would show the Europeans that the Sublime Porte was not against the proposal to implement reforms in Armenia and that it really wanted to do so, but that there was an enormous difficulty to overcome the bigotry of the Kurds and the Muslim masses in general, whose religion and customs resisted any reforms whatsoever. It wanted to show that if the government went against the will of the Muslim people, it would provide the opportunity for a great massacre of Christians, which the Sublime Porte found difficult to take responsibility for.

How illusory these suppositions were may be understood by anyone who has some knowledge of the state of Asiatic Turkey. The Muslims are as repressed and exploited by a disorganised government as the Christians are. The Muslims also want a good government; this may be illustrated by the as-yet unsettled rebellions by the Mountefig Arabs and Ghozan Tazlis, as well as by the reforms demanded by Midhat Pasha for Syria that were stubbornly refused by the Sublime Porte.

Muslim bigotry is a tool always used by the Sublime Porte to try to frighten Europe. Much is said about reforms and autonomy in Armenia, with many explanations given by the Sublime Porte; but the Kurds have as much knowledge of these negotiations as the wolves that inhabit the mountains of Armenia. Everything is talked about, fixed and arranged in Constantinople; how can the Kurds be interested in the autonomy of Armenia or the reforms that are supposed to be introduced there? The Kurd neither reads newspapers nor knows what is happening beyond the mountains in which he lives.

In spite of this, the Sublime Porte finds it expedient to present a Kurdish Union. If it did not exist, it would have been necessary to state that it could be formed, as the Turkish newspaper *Osmanli* supposed.

Could it really be formed? To answer that question, we consider it necessary to provide some idea of what sort of people the Kurds are.

Of the primitive peoples still living in the east, none retains as much as the Kurds the way of life their herdsmen forefathers led in centuries past. There is no people in the east that is so divided into tribes as the Kurds. In Vasbouragan[65] alone, there are over 120 individual tribes differing from one another in terms of dialect, customs and even religion. Those tribes have nothing in common, and no common link; each tribe lives separately, with its narrow, limited life. If one tribe's interests impinge on another's, it provokes bitter enmity between them. Resentment and the seeking of blood-revenge permeates them, from one generation to the next.

As a pastoral and nomadic people, the Kurds (even until today) have not learned to live a settled life. Their homeland is wherever there is grazing for their animals. For that reason, they migrate from one place to another the whole year round.

They spend the spring, summer and autumn in the mountains of Armenia, while they migrate to warmer regions in winter, such as the provinces of Karmian and Hakkiari, the meadows on the eastern bank of the Tigris or the flatlands of Mesopotamia. There are tribes that stay in Armenia in winter, spreading themselves through Armenian villages and finding hospitality in Armenian houses. Real Kurdish villages, of which there are very few in Armenia, consist of underground hovels left empty for three out of four seasons. They are inhabited only in winter when, like moles, the Kurds seek shelter in the dark with their animals, impatiently awaiting the spring, when they can emerge from their lairs.

---

65. The area bordering the south-east of Lake Van.

In all of Armenia there's not one city or town that has any Kurdish inhabitants. What would the Kurd do in a town? He knows no trade, is not a merchant or trader, has no shop and does not enter domestic service. The Kurd is a shepherd, and his home is the mountains, valleys and deserts.

All the Turkish government's efforts to make the Kurds settle in houses have been fruitless. The Turkish government uses all the means at its disposal to make the Kurds landowners and agriculturalists, but the Kurd dislikes land. They may tie him to it, but he wants to be free and migrate constantly. The robber cannot stay in one place very long.

As we have said, there are very few Kurdish villages in Armenia, and those are used for winter residence only. Just as swiftly as those villages are founded, so are they destroyed and left in ruins. Kurdish villages and their movable "opas" are all alike. A group of Kurds may be seen in a valley with their "alatchoughs": they remain there while there is pasture. Immediately, when it is finished, they pack their tents and move to another valley. This is how Kurds create their "gheshlaghs": they excavate the ground, cover it with bushes and brushwood, and their quarters are ready. The next winter they do the same thing elsewhere.

The Kurds in Armenia (with notable exceptions) do not possess land or fixed assets. If they own a piece of land, they give it to Armenians to till. Circumstances sometimes force them to leave the place where they are living, and they forget their piece of land as easily as they obtained it.

From all this, it is easy to see that the Kurds do not have a homeland; they are not tied by anything to Armenia, as they constantly migrate from Persia to Turkey and vice versa.

The Kurds have never been, nor can they be, friends with the Turks. Although during the last Russo-Turkish war several groups of Kurds mixed with Turkish *bashi-bozouks* [irregular troops] with the aim of obtaining loot, when the Turks were being beaten, the Kurds were the first to start pillaging their army. The Turkish soldiers' best weapons, obtained thanks to the British, were stolen in vast quantities by the Kurds and sold in Persia for rock-bottom prices.

The idea, widely spread, that the Kurds are a brave people is false. The Kurds, like all wild tribes, are not brave in the true sense of the word. To be really brave one must be inspired by some ideal. But the Kurd does not have any ideals. What can make the Kurd spill blood other than the desire for pillage?[66] That sort of bravery is that of an animal, when it is after prey. If the Kurd is beaten or massacred once, he loses his courage.

Throughout the centuries, the Kurds in Armenia have not been able to form a community, set down roots and be linked to the country through their own interests. The Kurds are not citizens of Armenia; they are migrants, like the gypsies of the area, beasts, Turkmen, Circassians, and other wild tribes who are here one day and gone the next, leaving no trace of their passing. From all this it is easy to see how practical the idea of a Kurdish Union is.

The establishment of a Kurdish Union in Armenia is impossible, but one thing may happen: Turkish government agents may stir up various Kurdish chieftains or this or that sheikh to rob Armenian villages. The Kurds would do that, provided they are permitted to carry out robberies unpunished. They'd begin to rob, burn and kill, and all the barbarities carried out in Armenia would be given a political appearance in Constantinople. As recently as the autumn of last year (1879) Sheikh Ibatullah, crossing the border from Persia into Turkey, once more destroyed up to 20 Armenian villages in the counties of Aghpag and Bashkale. That was simply a raid, the like of which happens in Armenia every year, but it was given a political character in Constantinople.

The same can happen from now on. Turkish government agents secretly stir the Kurds against the Armenians and massacres begin. Meanwhile, the Turkish press and the Sublime Porte begin to shout "This is the Kurdish Union. You see? The massacre happened because demands were made for autonomy for the Armenians." The Kurds, of course, know nothing about reforms or autonomy in Armenia; they are not capable of understanding what reforms are. They carry

---

66. The word used here can denote depredation, usurpation, pillage, raping, kidnapping, robbery, plunder, spoil or extortion.

out their barbarities, as always, simply for loot, but the Turkish government ascribes to them a political agenda.

One way or other, there is no great difference. Does the Kurd act knowingly or instinctively? In one way or another, the difference is not great. It all ends the same way: massacre in Armenia. There is plenty of proof already available. Yesterday there was a telegram from the British consul in Van, informing Constantinople that the Kurds have destroyed 13 Armenian villages.

We have to ask: what are they to do in such circumstances? Up to the present time, when the Kurds were committing robbery, arson and murder, the Armenians approached the Turkish government to demand judicial proceedings. But now, when the government agents themselves are encouraging the Kurds to commit barbarities, to whom can the Armenians appeal for justice? The answer we receive is: Europe, which has taken it upon itself to oversee Armenian reforms. But until Europe examines the situation and understands the events that have taken place in Armenia—until it reaches out to help (will it help?)—"the water will come and sweep away the watermill", as they say.

The Armenians understand this very well. They have understood that a critical moment has been reached when either they must slavishly accept the fact of being destroyed, or, if they want to preserve their identity, they must resist the savage Kurdish attacks with a united force. There is no other way. It is for that reason that groups of armed Armenians were formed whose aim was not rebellion—not to fight against the Turkish government—but to punish the Kurds if they dare to upset the peace of the country and rob the unarmed Armenian peasantry. Those armed groups, whose number is not small, move around the Armenian mountains, watch movements and take revenge wherever they see cruelties perpetrated by Kurds.

The armed Armenian groups even protect peace-loving Kurdish tribes when the latter become targets of barbarities by other tribes. It is for that reason that many Kurds have joined the Armenians and find it better to fight the common enemy than to hurt the Armenians, who have always helped and trusted them.

Brave Assyrians under their notable Mar-Shimon, the powerful prince and patriarch[67] of the Cholamerig mountains, have joined the Armenian armed groups; they have not been able to forget the great blow that befell their patriarchal house when, during the previous Mar-Shimon's reign, the tyrant of Bohdan (a Kurdish bandit by the name of Badir-Khan-Beg) robbed him of everything and killed up to 10,000 Assyrians. From that day, unceasing enmity exists between the Kurds and Mar-Shimon's tribe, often resulting in bloodshed. Only two years ago, when the Kurds attacked a few villages in Cholamerig and stole the patriarch's herd of mules from the meadow, the Assyrians, killing many of the Kurds, retrieved their animals. Always having clashes with the Kurds, Mar-Shimon has 30,000 to 40,000 armed men ready, even in peacetime; now all the Armenians and Assyrians in Cholamerig are armed.

Last year's famine, with its dreadful results, was also a tremendous help to the Armenian movement. During the famine, the Armenians clearly saw the maliciousness of the Turkish officials who did everything in their power to increase the number of Armenians who died of starvation. From that time, the Armenians were even more deeply convinced that Turkey wanted to permanently eliminate them. It was from that time that the idea of self-defence was born among them.

The famine had other benefits. It morally linked all Armenian hearts, and Armenians from all parts of the world began to send their munificent gifts there. The famine promoted peace between the Armenians and several Kurdish tribes, who received equal help from the Armenian aid committees that had been set up in the cities and towns of Armenia to aid those suffering from famine. Finally, thanks to the famine, during the spring of this year, a vast number of peasants from Van, Moush, Paghesh and Old Bayazid moved to Russia and spread throughout the trans-Caucasian provinces. Those

---

67. The Nestorian Assyrian Patriarchate is hereditary. All the patriarchs are elected from the same house and are called 'Mar-Shimon', or Lord Simon. (Author's note)

peasants, hearing of the danger to Armenia, are now returning to their homeland.

The current movement among the Turkish Armenians is a fact; it is the emphatic result of centuries of dreadful repression and the terrible expression of historical imperatives. The only way that Turkey can stop the movement is by carrying out the just Armenians' demands. But as the Turks are trying to kill off the Armenian Question through the invention of a Kurdish Union, the just rage of the Armenians will only increase.

THE KURD AND THE TURK[68]

Although Daron and Vasbouragan form part of Turkey, various Kurdish tribes, taking advantage of the weakness of the Sultan's government, rule those two large provinces of Armenia that cover an area from the south-eastern shore of the Black Sea and the Euphrates to Mesopotamia and the borders with Persia.

Daron and Vasbouragan contain the regions of Hakkiari, Bayazid, Haghpag, Van, Paghesh (Bitlis), Moush, Shadakh, Sassoun, Khizan, Mogk, Charsandjak and Keghi, etc., which are ruled by the Kurds.

The remaining resident nationalities, apart from the Kurds, include Armenians, Assyrians, Jews, Turks, Yezedis and various nomadic tribes. The Armenians, due to their large numbers, make up almost half of the total population of the provinces.

To grasp the situation the Armenians of the two provinces are in, it is necessary to understand the nature and political organisation of the ruling race, the Kurds.

The Kurds are divided into various tribes, the most important of which are the Moukouri, Tagouri, Milatsni, Haydaranli, Shavi, Tchalali, Ravand, Pilpasd, Mamekani, Hartoshi, Shigag, Harki and Yezedi. They differ only slightly in their particulars and customs. They speak a Median language, with each tribe speaking a different dialect. In terms of religion they are largely Muslims, of the Sunni sect; only the Yezedis differ from them in religion and worship good and evil spirits and the house hearth. It is possible that they are the remnants of the people who used to worship the pagan gods Aramazt and Arhmni, and among whom pagan rites still appear.

---

68. "Koorta Yev Toorka", *Mshak*, 1875.

The Kurds do not have a written language or literature. Their sheikhs know how to read only Arabic, and this they use to teach the commands of their faith to the people, including a few simple, external forms of worship. The only thing that every Kurd knows about his faith is the way to pray, which they do at set hours, without understanding the meanings of the devoutly recited Arabic words. Apart from that, the Kurd knows the great prophet's name (Mohammed), the names of the previous caliphs (Omar, Osman and Abu-Bakr), and nothing more.

Popular oral poetry is alive among the Kurds. It was born of the real life of the masses and has the same nature and spirit as the people from which it sprang. Pastoral and noble rhapsodies hold the main places in their poetry, the first as the expression of a pastoral people, the second reflecting their war-like character. The pastoral songs are sad and melancholy and are very gently harmonised with the attractive tones of the flute. The warlike songs, on the other hand, are fiery, bright and proud, and are sung with great confidence and verve, roaring with the sound of the drum.

No important event is lost in the life of the Kurd. Popular spirit either glorifies someone's brave deeds or criticises another's weakness in its songs. If someone hides from his enemy or flees the field of battle, the women and girls create various songs expressing reprehension the very next day, and they spread from one person, be it a child or adult, to the next.

The sword, a brace of pistols, a shield and a spear are part of his physical being, always inseparable from him. He uses a rifle in large battles, and his saddled horse, always ready in front of his tent, is the Kurd's faithful friend. (He loves it more than his wife or children). In his tent the Kurd is as hospitable as Abraham, but has no compunction in robbing that same guest if he were to meet him a mile away from it. Blood vengeance—as in all half-wild tribes like the Kurds—passes from one generation to the next; a murdered corpse cannot rest easy in its grave until bloody vengeance has been exacted from the killer or his near relations. The killer is only free from vengeance if he goes to his enemy's house, puts his sword under his feet and asks for forgiveness. It is very rarely that a Kurd will lower himself this much, as the Kurd is vengeful and hostile. Until the day he dies, he will never forget a slight or offence that goes without satisfaction. At the same time, in many circumstances, he is proud and noble: the Kurd will stop fighting when women from his enemy's side intercede. He does not lower himself by fighting with weak beings, although the Kurdish woman is just as fierce and bravehearted in battle as her husband.

For a Kurdish woman, a second marriage upon the death of her husband is anathema. She always remains a widow, consoling herself with sweet memories: that her husband was a "good bandit", always remained unblemished by timidity, and never showed his back to his enemies; that he loved his wife as much as he loved his Arabian horse; and that he was never attracted by the most beautiful girls of the tribe. A widowed mother would tell her children to follow him and once more raise his memory from the depths of the grave.

From childhood, the Kurd is taught to handle horses and weapons, and learns about physical exercise and other skills. He considers robbery and pillage brave acts, taking through them what is necessary for his living. He even steals his future wife—marriage is considered lucky when the hero kidnaps the girl he loves from her father's family. Under those circumstances, the girl can look upon her female friends with a special pride.

The greatest oath a Kurd can make is on the *talakh*. He takes a stone and, throwing it, says, "May my talakh be thrown like this stone, if I do this or that." (The talakh is his marriage vow, and he is considered divorced if, having made the oath, he betrays it). That sort of oath is demanded when, in any activity, the most solemn pledge is needed about the trustworthiness of another person. It is made when the activity concerned is most important for the community as a whole.

As the free son of nature, wedded to his carefree and simple life, the Kurd is satisfied with his animals. He is a shepherd, and he has no house or settled home. His shelter is his tent, pitched where he can find pasture for his animals. Only the winter weather drags the Kurd away from his beloved mountains, when an Armenian house is always ready to welcome the uninvited guest. The Kurd spends the winter there with his animals, until the spring calls him once more to his mountains.

The Kurd's diet comprises milk, yoghurt, cheese, cream, butter and fat from his animals. He never eats their meat. From head to foot, he is dressed in clothes made from the leather and wool of his animals, all made by his wife. A Kurd does not have much to do with the running of the house; he's a warrior. Cultivation or a skilled trade are activities beneath him, and he treats them with contempt, considering them work to be done by *rayah*s. Trade is carried on in the old way, by barter. The Kurd gives, for example, 20 sheep for a horse. He exchanges his fat, cheese and wool for the cultivator's flour or for this or that tool made by an artisan. All this is done with the greatest ingenuousness: in every transaction he is cheated, with the Armenian or Jewish merchant trying to make the maximum profit possible. This works, because in such cases of communication, the Kurd does not use his sword or physical strength, which are well developed; instead, he uses his knowledge and intelligence—which, in him, are poor.

The Kurd is not a cheat; he faithfully fulfils his promises. He pays what he owes for something he bought and steals someone else's property; both things are sacred to him. In the first case, he retains his honour and his word, and in the second his right and justice—for a Kurd, nothing is against what is right and just, when he has taken possession of something by his sword and the strength of his victory. The sword and victory are the scales of justice between him and his opponent.

Every bandit acts like this; so does every community of the same nature, as does the government of every country that takes on the role of a bandit.

Considering that this is enough about the Kurd's nature and family life, let us turn to the organisation of his political life.

Kurdish tribes are ruled by their *el-aghasi*s (tribal leaders) and sheikhs (religious leaders).

The tribal leader, who's called "Mir" (lord), is not appointed according to electoral principles. As the patriarch of the tribe, he rules by descent, from one generation to the next. The whole tribe submits to his rule with humility and filial obedience. The tribesman's sword, his hand and his life are at the service of the chieftain's will and pleasure, no matter how bad or barbaric they may be. It is the tribal leader who adjudicates on tribal disputes, distributes loot among the looters, leads his men into battle and sends out groups on pillaging expeditions. Every day, sitting in his tent, he receives the tribe's notable men who, fully armed and accoutred, present themselves to their chief to hear his orders. There they each smoke the chibukh of hospitality and drink a cup of bitter coffee. This "salaam" takes place regularly every morning.

Sheikhs are chosen from the main religious leaders. The tribes have their own muftis and kadis. The sheikhs cater to the tribe's religious needs, such as marriages, circumcisions and community prayer meetings; they go into battle as regular soldiers, but lead looting forays. In any event, they enjoy the esteem of the tribe to the extent of the religious feelings that a simple, half-wild people (like the Kurds) have.

The whole of the provinces of Daron and Vasbouragan are divided among the various Kurdish tribes. In each tribal area land is distributed, with each recipient given a portion to rule over, from the largest to the smallest.

The rayah (or subject) pays various taxes to till the land; to have animals and a trade; on his place of residence; and a head tax. In other words, there is a tax on everything that is pertinent to the necessities of his life and living. There are no limits to the amounts or weight of the taxes levied; that depends on the recipient's conscience. The people who are entitled to be lords of the rayahs and have permission to demand taxes are called khafir or derebeys; within the tribe, they are noble men of some importance. For example, the tribal chieftain has relatives or people who carry out his orders, so he gives to each one or more villages to secure their living. People like them therefore receive khafir rights. In their turn, his relatives or officers have servants—each of whom, instead of wages, are given perhaps a village or one or more families as their source of income. Those servants, relatives or officers treat the families assigned to them as their own property or subjects. This is how the divisions of the country descend from the largest part to that of a single family.

Authority flows down in stages from the chieftain to the lowest servant, as do the rights to ownership, starting from the largest portions of the land to the smallest.

The country is not, however, the family patrimony of the aghas (khafirs) or inherited land, but their possessions by conquest. It is for that reason that the land continually passes from one ruler to another, depending on whose sword is the most powerful.

In this way, the battles among rulers become permanent and never-ending.

During such wars, the settled population belonging to each side—be it in victory or defeat—suffers terribly. For example, a tribe wants to steal this or that part of the country from another tribe, and so it either rules the land by conquest or returns to its own lands, looting everything it can lay its hands on. Under these circumstances, the settled population leaves its homes and fields and, to save itself, seeks safety in inaccessible places in the mountains. The battles last for a long time. The animals, now ownerless, are stolen by the enemy. The harvest, being left, dries up and dies. After those battles, another and more terrible enemy emerges—famine.

The people are permanently in a state of fear and hopelessness. They do not know whether they will be at peace tomorrow, as the enemy is always ready, as they say, at their back. If, during the storms created by wars, they lose the fruits of their agriculture, the next day they will have no bread to eat, as they do not keep provisions for the future. (Firstly, because they have no safe place to store any and, secondly, because their extra weight would prevent their escape from enemy hands, when all they want to do is to save themselves).

The fighting and the continuous transfer of the population from one ruler to another consume the inhabitants by means of sword, fire and famine.

Suddenly, the former ruler considers himself beaten. So, to prevent the victor from enjoying the spoils, he burns all the villages, destroys the towns and sets fire to the ripening crops and fields; he leaves the entire region that belonged to him a desert, and then leaves. In these circumstances, the Kurd loses nothing, because he is a temporary guest, while all the buildings that have been consumed by fire belonged to Armenians or other foreign inhabitants and the fruits of cultivation were the results of their efforts. The attacker acts in the same barbaric way. When he sees that he cannot rule the attacked area, he escapes from the field of battle, leaving ruin and desolation behind him.

The people are always in a situation like that of a bird whose nest has been destroyed by a naughty child, and who sits on a swaying twig, not knowing what to do. The inhabitant has no heart to rebuild his cottage, because he wonders if he'll be able to live in it for very long. He has no heart to sow his field again, as there is no hope of reaping a harvest. All his movable possessions are always buried in the ground or in specially-constructed, underground store-cupboards so that, when he has to escape, they will not fall into enemy hands. But does he succeed in bringing out his possessions from their grave again? Not often, as frequently the person who hid them, meeting the enemy, is denied life and the secret of his cupboards goes with him to the next world. It is for that reason that in Armenia even today, when digging, so many brass and iron articles and pieces of women's jewellery are found. They are things buried during fighting, whose owners have been laid to rest with them.

This is the Armenians' situation in Daron and Vasbouragan. Their misfortune is in the fact that the ruling tyrant—the Kurd—is not the owner of the land, but a mob composed of wandering tribes which, like a fierce storm, moves from one end of the country to the other, destroying as it goes all life and everything that has been produced by industrious hands.

The Kurd does not have governmental ambitions, nor is the pride of creating an empire understandable to him. He looks at the people he conquers as he looks at the grass in the mountains where his animals graze: the people provide the Kurd with his needs; the pasture provides food for his flocks and herds. He does not tend to the latter so that it will increase; nor does he think about looking after the people, either. The Kurd is certain that, as his sword cuts and his arms move, everything is there for him and he will always find good pastures.

In the provinces of Daron and Vasbouragan, apart from the mutual hostility among the Kurds, there are attacks from external enemies. It happens not a little that after the offensives, the battles end with fire, blood, hostage-taking and looting. In these sorts of cases, it is the settled population that is in danger; the Kurds, if they have not the strength to resist the enemy, will retreat to inaccessible places in the mountains and wait until the enemy departs.

It often happens that Ottoman government soldiers are sent to pacify the country's border and conquer rebellious Kurds. The Turkish soldier behaves in the same barbaric way as the Persians. This is because Turkish rule either does not succeed or, if it does, it is only temporary; the soldier, not to return empty-handed, steals whatever he comes across.

All these provinces are in roughly the same situation—those being Erzerum, Bayazid, Haghpag, Van, Paghesh, Moush, Shadakh, Sassoun, Khizan, Mogk, Charsandjak and Kghi—along with their many Armenian inhabitants. They are ruled by bandit tribes, the individual tribesmen having one hand on the sword and his horse ready, and whose home is a light tent. His homeland is anywhere, his harvest is wretched people, his laws and rights are his will, his life's aim is total destruction, and his working spirit is his inhuman heart, wild rage and animal boldness.

THE ESCAPE ROUTE[69]

A telegraph brought us the news that the Sublime Porte, in its answer to the European ambassadors, has promised to persuade the Albanians to cede Tultsino to Montenegro, to undertake to solve the Greek problem in three months and settle the Armenian Question in four.

This is yet another dark, two-faced and cunning answer which the Sublime Porte has the habit of using to avoid actually carrying out the demands of Europe, to find an escape route, and prepare new difficulties and gain time to create new obstacles.

The Sublime Porte undertakes to resolve the Armenian Question in four months, but how? What reforms will it introduce into Armenia? On this issue, it is silent.

Bearing in mind the events that are now taking place in Turkish Armenia, it is very easy to guess how the Sublime Porte will resolve the Armenian Question in this four month period.

It will, like it did before, send commissioners and reformers like Hobart Pasha to Armenia, thus showing that it is trying to introduce reforms; at the same time, however, they will secretly inflame the Kurds and the whole of the Muslim population against the Armenians. Instead of reforms, it will spread blood, massacre and destruction throughout Armenia. Four months is enough to do all that.

When Armenia is drenched in blood and flames, it will reply to Europe: "My people are not ready. I tried everything. It is impossible at present to introduce reforms into Armenia, because the religious

---

69. "Pakhousti Janabara" (posthumous), written in 1880, first published in Tiflis in *Tajgahayk*, 1895.

feelings of the Muslim mob are inflamed and Turkish national pride is hurt due to the privileges offered to the Armenians."

Making promises but not keeping them—that is Turkey's ancient habit. To promise good and yet do evil—that is what its present thoroughly fraudulent policies demand.

It is understandable that the Sublime Porte will use every wile to prevent the implementation of Article 61 of the Treaty of Berlin in Armenia. It understands very well what that Article promises for the Armenian people.

The name "Armenia" touches a raw nerve with the Turks. The Sublime Porte declared to the Armenian Patriarch, in no uncertain terms, that it recognised no land within its borders called Armenia. It told the European ambassadors that it had no intention of introducing reforms in Armenia specifically, but will introduce reforms in all of Asia Minor generally. What do these words mean? It is very easy to see that the Sublime Porte does not want Armenia to become a legitimate[70] country, to be autonomous and secede from it. The Turks cannot, of course, easily forget the history of the creation of governments on the Balkan peninsula.

Without taking into account that Armenian aims are very modest or that the Armenians only want a benevolent government and freedom from the barbarities visited on them for centuries (until the present day) by Muslims, the Sublime Porte does not wish to grant their just demands, the sort of demands which the citizen of any more or less orderly country has the right to enjoy.

That's not enough: now, Turkey is trying to kill off the Armenian Question by killing off the Armenian element of the population. It is attempting to fill Armenia with Kurds, Circassians, Lazes and Ajars and stir up the barbarity of all those wild tribes against the Armenians. Turkey has settled in Armenia all the Muslims, who have emigrated from the provinces captured by the Russians—and groups of refugees from European Turkey have been sent, in the same way, to Armenia.

The aim is obvious and four months is long enough to complete the plan.

---

70. The word used here is 'ardonagan': licensed, authorised, permitted etc.

The signs are already obvious in Vasbouragan, the Armenian heartland, where violent Kurdish feelings are evident. Villages are being burnt, people are being murdered and raids are spreading and becoming ever more threatening. Blood is flowing in the same way in Daron. In the province of Sovough-Boulagh, Sheikh Ibatullah, with his more than 10,000 bandits, is a threat to the Armenians of Aderbadagan.[71] Bahri-Beg, at the head of his tribe, is wreaking destruction in the Hakkiari region. In the Old Bayazid region, the Haydaranli Kurds are robbing Armenians. The same evils are to be seen everywhere, and beneath the surface are the hidden hands of the Turkish government's cunning agents. At the same time, the Turkish press in Constantinople is explaining all these barbarities away in the name of the Kurdish Union.

How shall the Turkish Armenians act in response to all these evils?

The Turkish Armenians have, until today, placed all their hopes on diplomatic negotiations, expecting everything from Europe and looking for their salvation to Article 61 of the Treaty of Berlin. But a British official, Mr Bryce, recently (in 1880) told the Armenians of Constantinople with great clarity: "Try not to bore Europe."

We would like to add something to the British armenophile's words: not only Europe, but God Himself will not help the Turkish Armenians, if they are lax in helping themselves.

Turkey has promised to solve the Armenian Question in four months. That solution may well be that in four months time there will be no Armenians left in Armenia.

---

71. The area in present day Iran located between Lake Urmia and the Caspian Sea known as Persian Azerbaijan.

LET US HELP[72]

When various Armenian organisations were set up in Constantinople—such as "Araratian", "Giligian" and "Tbrotsasiradz Arevelian"—with the aim of spreading education in Armenia, many of us began to think: "What is the use of having so many organisations? Is not the aim the same? Would it not be better if they all united and formed a single and more basic organisation?"

These thoughts are justified. The abovementioned organisations are based on benevolent principles and can only exist with donations. But the Armenian community does not know to which of them it should provide monetary assistance. All of them are doing the same thing and working to achieve the same aim.

The Armenians of Constantinople, who had greater hopes and expectations from us, the Russian Armenians, in terms of financial assistance, have of course not only agreed with us on the unification of the various organisations, but have actually carried out our hope that they do so. Announcements have appeared in the press to the effect that those organisations had united under the name of "United Organisations".

What remains for us to do now?

Now we must redouble our benevolent energy, giving United Organisations strength and encouragement by providing financial assistance.

Each of us is convinced that learning and education are the main ways by which Turkish Armenians will create a basic road to future happiness, albeit a little late and slowly. We are convinced that the

---

72. "Nbastenk" (posthumous), written in 1880, first published in *Tajgahayk*, Tiflis 1913.

Turkish Armenian will find his renaissance and good fortune in school. Armenian children will receive, from the hands of their teachers, those benefits that the Armenians have been denied until today by barbarian Turkey and which European diplomats are slow in spreading.

But Turkish Armenians are poor; the oppression visited on them by the Turks has so squeezed their financial resources that it is difficult for them to maintain and make their schools prosper in a regular, proper manner, unless aid reaches them from outside Turkey.

Russian Armenians must do for the Turkish Armenians what they once did with gold for all the Armenians of India. The Russian Armenians, living under the protection of a benevolent government, are in a more affluent financial state than their Turkish Armenian brothers.

The Indian Armenians left important wills to the nation; many schools were founded in various countries by way of their bequests. It would be wonderful if we could follow their example, but our demands are modest; we do not demand the benefits of sizeable wills.

There would be no financial effect for any of us if we were to put a moral debt on ourselves every year, according to our means, to provide a gift to United Organisations of Constantinople of a few roubles. From those roubles great sums could be accrued.

The Russian Armenians showed their benevolent energy to the "Araratian" organisation and how much they sympathised with the advancement of education in Turkish Armenia. We have the hope that they will increase their sacrifices many times over when a magnificent, basic organisation is formed from the various individual ones.

* * *

The Russo-Turkish war began in the name of freedom for Christians; the Armenians, instead of using red blood, used black ink to achieve Article 16 of the Treaty of San Stefano and Article 61 of the Treaty of Berlin. According to the wording of the latter, Turkey was obliged to introduce reforms into the "provinces inhabited by Armenians". A question naturally arises: who are the Armenians?

In the opinion of our older notables, only those belonging to the Armenian Apostolic faith (Lousavorchagans or Gregorians) are

Armenians; Turkey was "benevolent" enough to accept that, and so counted the number of Apostolic Armenians, thus reducing the total number; Turkey replied to Europe that the Armenians are such a small minority that it was not worth making reforms specifically for them. That answer, from the point of view of religion, was partially correct. None of us has the right to censure Turkey when it repeats the same thing that we have said, which was that, apart from the adherents of Apostolic Armenians (Lousavorchagans), there were no other Armenians.

It is obvious to all what severe consequences there may be for reforms if we continue to repeat that outside of the Armenian Apostolic Church there are no Armenians. (The subject of religion and nationality has been raised for this reason).

Article 61 of the Treaty of Berlin gave the Armenians two rights: first, that reforms must be introduced into Armenia and, second, that the religious community of Armenians was recognised before Europe as a nation.

What does the change from religious community to nation mean? It means a racial whole, in which there are and may be various religions and churches.

To be worthy of the name, it must be demonstrated that this is the case—that we are a nation, and that there are various churches within the nation: Armenian Apostolic, Protestant, Catholic, Greek Orthodox and Muslim. Given that form of organisation, religious tolerance and freedom of conscience would necessarily and spontaneously emerge, thus bringing the work of national unity to perfection.

This desirable union has been canvassed for a very long time. After the signing of the Treaty of Berlin, it was put forward with greater zeal, as a union was seen to be the salvation of the nation and Armenia's fortune and future. But people were found who began to preach the opposite, or to explain our ideas in an incorrect or crooked way. We have nothing to do with such individuals; we are involved with our nation's sincere friends. We will continually whip those villains, whether they be Catholic, Armenian Apostolic, Protestant, Greek Orthodox or Muslim, and who introduce difficulties into the work of unifying the nation. We embrace, with pleasure and without touching on their religion, our brothers who work in the name of Armenians and Armenia, and who defend Armenian interests.

We are all sons and daughters of one nation and members of the same family. Religion, which once divided us, must be supplanted as a unifying force in favour of a love of nation and country. Catholicism, protestantism and even Islam do not preclude Armenians from being Armenian; neither does being Apostolic Armenian give us the right to call ourselves Armenians. We were Armenian when we were pagans and will remain Armenian even if we change our religion a thousand times. We will not lose our nationality, and all the necessary conditions exist for the survival of a nation.

RAFFI

ARMENIA'S FOREMOST NOVELIST

Authentic, first rate translations into English

*www.gomidas.org * info@gomidas.org*

www.ingramcontent.com/pod-product-compliance
Lightning Source LLC
Chambersburg PA
CBHW031157160426
43193CB00008B/403